BUILDERS OF NEW ENGLAND

By Shirley Barker

Author of THE STRANGE WIVES, *etc.*

Illustrated with photographs

BEFORE THERE WERE ever New Englanders, there was the land—an area of granite hills and wooded valleys, salt marshes, pine and oak forests, mountain peaks, river intervals and ragged shores. A wilderness country of Indian hunting grounds, it covered most of the territory east of the Hudson, south of Canada and west of Nova Scotia, with the wide, ever-changing carpet of the Atlantic Ocean spread before its front door. From across the ocean to this land and out of it came an extraordinary group of men whose careers helped to forge the New England states and thereby the nation. Statesmen, engineers, farmers, frontiersmen, craftsmen, men of God, all of them were patriots and most were soldiers who fought actively at one time or another for their freedom.

Shirley Barker, whose books include several on historical subjects, revives the life and spirit of twelve of these men who are representative of the builders of New England: Governors Bradford and Winthrop, Roger Williams, Cotton Mather, Jonathan Edwards, Paul Revere, John Hancock, John Adams, Ethan Allen, John Stark, Samuel Morey, and Eli Whitney. Each in his own way left the stamp of his influence indelibly imprinted on the New England scene, and his story is an integral part of American history.

BUILDERS OF NEW ENGLAND

Shirley Barker

BUILDERS OF
NEW ENGLAND

ILLUSTRATED

DODD, MEAD & COMPANY

NEW YORK

Printed in the United States of America
by The Cornwall Press, Inc., Cornwall, N. Y.

TO THE MEMORY OF MY OWN BUILDER OF NEW ENGLAND
James Barker
a tailor of Suffolk
who came to Rowley, Massachusetts, in 1638

CONTENTS

CONTENTS

ILLUSTRATIONS

BUILDERS OF NEW ENGLAND

Chapter 1

———————❦———————

TWO COLONIAL GOVERNORS
William Bradford · John Winthrop

Before there were ever New Englanders there was New England. And now that in a sense there have ceased to be New Englanders, the country remains there still. Under the six-lane highways stretches the eternal granite that still makes up the craggy shores visited by Sir Humphrey Gilbert in the reign of Elizabeth I. After the neon lights go out above motel and amusement park, the stars shine down, here and there, on salt marshes and pine and oak forests, mountain peaks and river intervals, unchanged by the tides of human living that have surged around them in the last three hundred years. More and more we tend to become one people, Americans without local labels, as the magic carpet of modern transportation and communication brings Portland, Maine, and Portland, Oregon, ever closer together in thought as well as in actuality.

The country is here and can be viewed and studied, known and loved. What is popularly referred to as "the New England character" still survives in flashes of stubborn wit, wry twists

1

of humor, the lean habit of understatement, and a gnarled toughness of spirit that resists, not so much change, as any-thing at all which it cannot accept and approve of. But the early New Englanders, those who gave the term its signifi-cance, are gone with the world and the time that bred them. That they were worth knowing, everyone agrees, but many do not take the trouble to pursue the acquaintance until it ripens into understanding and friendship. To explore the possibilities of such acquaintance is the purpose of this book.

Let us go back in our minds to the year A.D. 1620. We have then New England as it was, a wilderness country of Indian hunting grounds, broken by occasional wigwam vil-lages and straggling maize fields. It covered most of the land east of the Hudson, south of Canada, and west of Nova Scotia, with the wide, everchanging carpet of the Atlantic Ocean spread before its front door. The land awaited. And on the other side of the ocean were rising up the men who would come to take this land and be taken by it, who would come to bear the name already given to it by the explorer Captain John Smith.

They grew up in an exciting England full of pageantry, expansion, and adventure, these first New Englanders. Eng-lish poets and playwrights were dedicating some of the finest literature of all time to England's most spectacular sovereign. Scholars were rediscovering the classics of antiquity, respond-ing to the Italian Renaissance. Great seamen like Sir Francis Drake shattered the Spanish fleet, explored the Caribbean, and brought rich treasures home. More money circulated over shop counters, and standards of living rose. The yeoman whose father had slept on a pile of rushes now lay in a wooden bedstead. The lad who hated to follow the plow could run off to sea, join a pirate crew, and come back with a velvet coat finer than Squire's and with money in his pockets. The merchants rose into a new richness and respectability as their ships ventured to far-off shores and returned with exotic merchandise. They could retire from trade now, buy up country houses, and marry aristocratic wives. Freedom of movement from a low social level to a higher one was now beginning. Democracy had not yet come about, but no one looked back any longer to feudalism. In this period of change, no changes were greater than those affecting the church.

English religious thinking had suffered a complete revolution during the last half of the sixteenth century. Within the Church of England a new group of men sprang up who came to be called "Puritans" because they sought ways of worshipping God that were "purer" than those their fathers had been content with. They objected to many abuses within the government of the church, but also to much of its ritual ceremony, such as the celebration of saints' days, even of Christmas, music in the churches, and the wearing of surplices by the clergy. They wanted their religious services to be starkly simple, offering no appeal to the senses that might divert men's souls from communion with God and the cultivation of piety.

They also wished to extend the sphere of religion further into daily life. Political and social conduct—even the clothes a man wore—should be subject to regulation by the clergy. They turned to the Bible as the true word of God and the source of all good. Man's behavior as a member of society should no longer be governed by English common law but by the law of Moses as laid down in the Bible. The object of all this was to make men lead purer lives to the glory of God, worship their Creator more devoutly, and thus prepare their souls for eternal salvation.

Naturally the established order resented the suggestion that it needed reform, and many of the clergy who embraced Puritanism were thrown out of their living.

But the movement exerted a strong appeal, and persecution only seemed to strengthen it. Slowly two types of Puritan emerged, the Separatists, and the Nonconformists. The Separatists wished to break off completely from the Church of England, to form separate churches, each one a single unit, a law unto itself. The Nonconformists, however, wished to bring about the desired reforms within the established church instead of withdrawing from it. As time went on, both groups came to feel that they would not be able to achieve their ideals in England and turned their eyes toward America, now open for English colonization. Perhaps, they thought, they might establish their pure new kingdom here, a true Bible commonwealth.

In 1620 the famous Pilgrims of Plymouth, a Separatist group, set out on their new world venture and founded the colony ably governed for years by William Bradford. In wild strawberry time, 1630, the Winthrop fleet sailed into Salem Harbor. Governor John Winthrop brought with him a sizable party of Nonconformists, more numerous, richer, better educated, and better supplied than their neighbors to the south. But it was a blend of both Nonconformist and Separatist principles that finally dominated Massachusetts and came to be called "the Congregational Way."

Not often did they meet together, these governors of the two separate colonies that eventually became the single state of Massachusetts. John Winthrop of the Bay Colony traveled constantly about the towns under his jurisdiction that looked to Boston as their capital. William Bradford ventured less often from Plymouth, since his was a simpler, more homespun operation, carried on with fewer resources and less display of authority. But they corresponded and occasionally visited each other, drawn by a mutual liking and respect and the necessity of discussing problems that concerned their governments.

One such meeting—not the first—took place in Bradford's house in Plymouth during the last week of October, 1632. The governor of Massachusetts Bay, tall, dark, aristocratic, with aquiline features and pride if not arrogance in his bearing, arrived on foot along the crooked coast road, accompanied by Pastor John Wilson and his military commander, Endicott. Bradford, in his long magisterial robes, turned out to meet his distinguished guests and led them to the small, square house with diamond-paned casement windows and low eaves which the Colony had set apart for him.

It stood behind its own fence at Plymouth's one crossroads, on the northwest corner of what are now Main and Leyden Streets, under the shadow of a sharp hill crowned by the palisaded fort and the burial ground. In the "old parlor," perhaps the first part of the house to be built, stood the wainscotted bed where Winthrop would sleep. In the "great room" the women and girls of Bradford's household were setting the rough-hewn trestle table with a turkey-red cloth, wooden and pewter dishes, a pair of cherished silver spoons. Iron kettles, which swung on poles over a brisk burning fire, held fragrant, simmering stews of wild game and harvest vegetables, seasoned with Mistress Bradford's favorite herbs—saffron, surely, perhaps rosemary, marjoram, and dill.

The two governors and their aides sat long at the table while darkness fell and the big stars brightened overhead. A chilly fall wind swirled the dead leaves about the house and rattled through the boughs of the somber oak trees. Winthrop stated his ideas for their mutual defense with forthrightness, courage, and brilliance. Bradford, mild, firm, of cheerful countenance, conscious of his visitor's superior wealth and university background, replied with deference but no lack of dignity. Perhaps he rose from time to time to throw wood on the dwindling fire. Perhaps both men, as they considered the problems of New England, paused more than once to gaze through the tiny panes at the dark waters of Plymouth Harbor. Beyond the harbor lay the great sea they had both come across. And beyond that lay the old home, the England they had both loved and to which they would never return. Their lives had lain far apart there and would diverge from this meeting to draw even further apart.

Having seen them thus together, let us now consider them as all men are finally considered, every one alone.

WILLIAM BRADFORD

Spring sunlight tempered with sudden rain lay on the Yorkshire moors and fens when William Bradford and his wife, the former Alice Hanson, carried their son to the church of St. Helen's in Austerfield for his baptism. March 19, 1590, it was, that the child received his father's and grandfather's name. And probably most folk in the tiny isolated village expected that he would grow up to live all his life in his family's square, stone house and tend their nearby farming lands, just as his father and grandfather had done.

The Bradfords had been sturdy, prosperous yeomen—free, landowning English farmers—for at least four generations, and the Hansons ranked little below them. It seemed unlikely that their child could ever come to want, unless through some thriftless errors of his own. Young William Bradford committed no thriftless errors, but his father's death when he was scarcely more than a year old thrust him into the care of his grandfather and uncles. They may have been kind to him. Certainly they saw that he got a tight thatched roof over his head and plenty of bread, cheese, and bacon, washed down with home-brewed ale. If they provided him with no education beyond the nearest grammar school, and perhaps not even that, they made sure that he knew all about plowing, planting, and harvesting, all the tedious, patient crafts so necessary in the country—setting hedge, pruning orchards, and shearing sheep.

As William grew from a sickly child into a hearty young man he spent much of his time tending the flocks, for the sale of wool and hand-woven woolen cloth accounted for most of the family's cash income. A scholarly lad for all his lack of opportunity, he knew the Bible thoroughly by the time he was twelve years old. Perhaps he carried it into the fields with him and read and studied and dreamed while his charges strayed. Perhaps it was here, or in the streets and lanes of the village, that he met the friend who took him first to hear the preaching of Richard Clyfton in the nearby hamlet of Babworth.

Richard Clyfton, "a grave, fatherly old man," preached the Puritan doctrines within the established church, and the young man from Austerfield found the tenets completely in tune with the religious convictions of his own heart. He went often to hear Clyfton although his uncles protested. When he was sixteen he joined the Separatist group in Scrooby whither Clyfton had removed, and here he met the two men who were henceforth as fathers to him, whose thinking led him over channel and ocean and ruled his whole adult life.

Lacking a proper church, the Scrooby group met in a small, half-ruined manor house, the home of William Brewster, a man more than twenty years older than the lad who plodded there faithfully every Sunday from Austerfield. Brewster had studied at Cambridge, held a minor position at court, and traveled in the Low Countries. But he had left the world of luxury and sophistication—and wickedness—to come back to the shire of his boyhood and serve as a country postmaster while he furthered the cause of the "purer" religion in which he fervently believed.

"He was wise and discreete and well spoken," Bradford wrote of him later, "having a grave and deliberate utterance, of a very cherfull spirite, very sociable and pleasante amongst his friends . . . inoffensive and innocent in his life and conversation . . . of an humble and modest mind . . . tender harted and compassionate of such as were in misery."

The young William must have been very devoted to the older one, seeing in him, perhaps, the father he had never known. Certainly he patterned himself on this new friend. The words with which Bradford describes him could as truthfully be spoken of Bradford himself by younger men who would know him at a later day. Very likely he had from Brewster the books and tutoring that provided him with the knowledge of history, languages, and the classics which his own writings displayed.

To Scrooby also came John Robinson, a noted Separatist

whom Bradford found "sharp of wit . . . of tender conscience
. . . an acute, able disputant, very profitable in his ministry
and comfortable to his people." Robinson believed strongly
in what we would think of today as the democracy of the
church: that all the congregation were alike in the eyes of
God and could make their own direct contacts with him. He
did not favor a state church or believe that any church could
be governed other than by its own members. He hated the
pomp and richness, the elaborate ceremonies and aristocracy,
of the Anglican priestly caste. A man could worship as well
kneeling humbly on bare boards before the Lord. Long after
his death his religious beliefs, carried overseas by the Plymouth Pilgrims, were built irrevocably into American political
philosophy. Perhaps it is for this reason that Plymouth remains a shrine for us today, more honored in history than
the other colonies, although Jamestown was earlier and the
Bay more powerful.

Under the leadership of Brewster, Clyfton, and Robinson the Scrooby group prospered briefly. Then Brewster was
arrested, fined, and gave up his postmastership. Throughout
the country other Separatists were being harried, imprisoned,
and executed. The time had come for the Lord's free people
to leave their familiar rooftrees and turn into wanderers and
pilgrims to preserve their faith. They went out of England,
and William Bradford went with them.

He traveled as a member of the Brewster household and
did not reach Holland with the first contingent, having stayed
behind to help convoy the women and children. On arriving
in August, 1608, he was arrested as a fugitive but managed
to extricate himself and get work with a French silkmaker.
Amsterdam was a fine, rich city in a peaceful, prosperous

country, with a respect for the rights of man and a tradition of religious freedom. A center of weaving, manufacturing, industry, and trade, it educated its children in state-supported schools and encouraged literature, art, and music. Beautiful mansions lined the banks of its many canals, but the Dutch burghers dressed plainly and encouraged thrift.

It was a strange world to the young man from the fields and farms of Yorkshire, used only to the countryman's simple routines of life. Many of Bradford's companions, too, were farmers and villagers who had never seen London, and they felt the strangeness as he did, the difficulty of learning city ways. Soon "the grim and grisely face of poverty" appeared among them.

Two earlier English congregations had settled in Amsterdam, but they were falling into disrepute, rocked with arguments and scandals. Brewster and Robinson soon decided to lead their followers to Leyden to set up their own permanent congregation, and they made the move in 1609. William Bradford went along with them as a matter of course, but his heart kept turning backward to Amsterdam where he had left the girl he would later marry, Dorothy May, in this year only a pretty child of eleven. In Leyden they bought land on one of the finest canals near the university. Gradually they built small homes for themselves, and when Bradford came into his English inheritance in 1611, he sold it and purchased a house where he could carry on his trade as a clothworker. To this house he brought his bride in December, 1613. Two years later she bore him a son, John.

The former Scrooby group had enlarged and achieved a small degree of prosperity, but many of the men still found it hard to earn a living by city crafts. They were essentially a country folk and longed for the security of their own fields around them. Trained in the Dutch schools, their children were taking on Dutch ways, and this distressed them. By 1619 it seemed that Holland might be drawn into war with Spain, and religious disputes arose which reminded them of the England to which they had no wish to return. Already their eyes were turning toward America, first to Virginia, then to New England. Bradford sold his house in that year and began to take an active part in consolidating the group's affairs for their removal, while Carver, Cushman, and Thomas Weston tried to make arrangements for London merchants to provide them with money.

From here on William Bradford's story is the story of Plymouth Colony, a tale too often told to need repeating. We know only too well how the little group gathered at Southampton after many difficulties, smelling for the last time the gorse on the wind of an English summer; how the *Speedwell* had to turn back while the others sailed on. We have shivered over the horrors of the long voyage in the tiny *Mayflower*, with late autumn winds troubling the bitter sea. We know that they did not land first at Plymouth, but within the curve of the bay near Provincetown; that they did not build four-square log cabins, but crude huts of clay, turf, or branches till the neat frame houses patterned after their English homes could be erected. We have suffered with them through that first winter of starvation and death. We have met their Indian friends, Massasoit, Hobomok, and Squanto, and joined in at their crude, bounteous feast on the first Thanksgiving Day.

Troubles beset them always. New immigrants came, hungry and needing shelter. The London adventurers supplied them but niggardly. Their fishing expeditions failed. Their shiploads of furs went to sea bottom or were captured by pirates. Yet they survived and built their plantation, only to see it dwindle away as their children struck out and took up new land, far from Town Brook and Burial Hill. The Bay Colony rose to the eastward, to overshadow and finally to absorb them. But they had persevered in their ideal and left an ideal for all America.

We know well the chief actors in the story: grave Governor Carver who died in the warmth of the first April, leaving Bradford to succeed him; steady, loyal Edward Winslow, wise beyond his years; scholarly Brewster; and treacherous Allerton. The wicked Billingtons, the immortal lovers John Alden and Priscilla, are household words among us. Even now, if we go to Plymouth on Thanksgiving Day we can see them impersonated by living men and women who march in their ancient costumes from the shore to the church halfway up the hill.

Bradford's own journal provides us with a vivid record of Plymouth's waxing and early wane, but it tells us not half as much as we could wish about Bradford the man. However we have glimpses of him—taken from the writings of other men—that help us to make him come alive.

Surely the poor Pilgrims had little to laugh about while they were exploring the frozen dunes round Truro that December of 1620, cutting their way through thorny woodlands that tore the armor of their fiery little red-haired warrior, Myles Standish. But they did laugh when William got his leg caught in a "pretie device" rigged up by the Indians to snare deer. He did not resent their laughter, may even have joined in it, but he probably watched his steps more carefully after that. He accompanied every exploring party and finally helped to choose Plymouth—"a place of diverse cornfields and little running brooks"—as best fitted for their settlement.

When he returned to the *Mayflower,* joyously eager to tell Dorothy that he had located a home for her where she could soon go ashore, he found that he had come too late. Dorothy was drowned in the sea. Was she swept overboard by a great wave? Did she fall from the deck by accident? Or had she seen enough of the forbidding shores, snow-clad and lashed with freezing wind, and taken her own way out? No one ever left a complete account of what happened, least of all her husband. Later he sent to England for an old acquaintance, the widow Alice Southworth, who came to him in 1623 with her two small sons. Alice made him a good wife, bore him children, and mothered Dorothy's child, John. Her house was always a refuge for the needy children of the colony, and she must have brought peace and happiness to her husband, by her tasks lightening his. And if he ever regretted the pretty girl he had courted amid the tulips of Amsterdam, he never said. It would not have been seemly, not the proper part of a man.

Nor did he have much time for personal grief among the grievous tasks of governing the colony. Reelected thirty times he was never out of office except when he begged off. Seeing everybody fed, housed, and reasonably law abiding, organizing fishing expeditions, settling land disputes, raising money pleading with the merchants in London, performing marriage ceremonies, dealing with the Indians and the nearby colonies, managing unruly visitors like John Oldham and Thomas Morton of Merrymount—these were all in the day's work for the former Yorkshire farm lad.

Gentle he could be, but bold and defiant when occasion

rose. When the Narragansetts sent him a snakeskin filled with arrows, he sent it back filled with musket balls, saying that if they wanted war they could begin whenever they would.

He had always been against the restriction imposed by the Londoners that the Plymouth settlers should hold everything in common, rather than each man working for himself, owning his own land, and improving it as he would. In 1623 he took the responsibility for assigning the common fields to individuals, and after this the colonists worked more diligently and with greater willingness, since it was to increase their private estates and provide a heritage for their children. Thus America's first experiment with communism came to an unlamented end.

In 1627 Bradford and a group of seven others among "the Old Comers" bought out what was left of the original founding company. They divided its possessions among the colonists and undertook to pay its debts, which they spent years in doing. In 1636 he took the lead in getting the laws of the colony written into an orderly code.

As time went on Bradford found himself more and more involved with the Bay Colony, trying to live in friendship and brotherhood with its leaders, to join them in policies for mutual good, but to keep his people from falling under the power of their severer laws and greater intolerance.

The 1640's brought him disillusionment. The young men were leaving Plymouth for the Cape or the fertile lands to the west. He sensed a falling off in piety and godliness. Prices fell, too, almost overnight, reducing men to paupers willy-nilly. Bradford husbanded their resources, reminded them of the leaner time of their beginnings, and struggled on.

In 1650 he entertained a strange guest for Puritan Plymouth. Father Gabriel Druillettes, a Roman Catholic priest who had been serving as a missionary to the Abenaki Indians along the Kennebec. Bradford had thoughtfully arranged for Dame Alice to provide a fish dinner, since it was Friday, and the two men sat down peacefully together, discussing their religious differences with mutual sympathy and understanding. Later they walked about the town and looked at the cannon by the fort, moss-grown now, never fired against either Indian or white man.

As Bradford grew older it troubled him that no permanent pastor had come to fill their pulpit, no man like John Robinson who had died long ago in Holland without ever following this part of his flock to the new country. He regretted, too, that opportunities for education still remained largely lacking to the children. Nor had anyone come forward to assist him with the burden of government. But he took things a little more easily now, rejoicing as his sons and stepsons grew to manhood and began to play men's parts; turning to his books again, writing poetry and studying Hebrew; still adding land to his holdings as became a good yeoman.

After a brief period of failing health, William Bradford died on the soft spring evening of May 19, 1657, disappointed in his colony's seeming decline, undervaluing the important work he had done. He left a personal estate rich in land but poor in money and valuables. His Plymouth house and lot were rated at only forty-five pounds. He left a "great silver beer bowle," two silver wine cups, thirteen spoons, four Venetian glasses, pewter dishes and flagons, and a library second only to Brewster's. And if sad-colored clothes hung in his wardrobe, so did a violet hat, a red coat, and a suit with silver buttons. Needless to say, his affairs were in good order.

His carefully kept journal, our best history of Plymouth Colony, went to his son. Taken back to England during the American Revolution, it was lost for a time and then discovered nearly a hundred years later in the palace of the Bishop of London and returned to America. Published under the title *Of Plimouth Plantation* it proves to be a storehouse of historical information but tells us little about the man, its author.

Men of Bradford's own time praised him for his dignity and wisdom, his cheerful countenance and loving kindness, his piety and his faithful care for little things, his temperateness, and his faithful years of toil to realize the ideal of a Christian community that he had kept before him from his youth.

"Thus out of smalle beginnings greater things have been prodused by his hand that made all things of nothing, and gives being to all things that are," he wrote. "And as one small candle may light a thousand, so the light here kindled hath shone to many, yea, in some sort to our whole nation; let the glorious name of Jehova have all the praise."

Not all the praise. Save some for Jehovah's instrument, William Bradford, the good shepherd who tended an infant colony in its weakness and thus helped to establish one of the finest traditions in American life.

JOHN WINTHROP

When John Winthrop sat down to dinner at William Bradford's humble cottage in Plymouth he was forty-four years old, senior to his host by a year or two. Never had he known the other's difficulties—the insecurity of an orphan childhood, the harried lot of a fugitive, the need to earn his bread by the work of his hands in a foreign city. Sober authority and a good store of material possessions had been his from his boyhood. But he had not come comfortably and unquestioningly to his religious faith as Bradford had. Often he was driven to search his own soul in doubt and anguish, and as often to discipline the cravings of the natural man. Bradford's trials and sufferings were of the flesh while Winthrop's were of the spirit.

His biographers begin with his grandfather, Adam Winthrop, who went to London to seek his fortune in the time of Henry VIII. He became a cloth merchant and prospered, so that by 1544 he was able to purchase Groton Manor near Bury St. Edmunds in Suffolk and set himself up as a country gentleman. It was a goodly estate in a gentle, rolling countryside, with fields for wheat, barley, and rye, woodlands and a shallow fishpond, a huge, timbered barn, and plenty of pasture land. Today only an ancient and twisted mulberry tree marks where the house stood, but it probably looked very much like the early New England houses, with a steep roof and gables, casement windows and leaded panes.

Adam's son—another Adam—took over in his time and administered his heritage well. As a young man he practiced law in London, grew rich, and acquired a coat of arms. On January 12, 1588, his second wife, Anne Browne, bore him a son, John, who would in his turn govern Groton Manor and relinquish it to seek wider acres across the sea.

The Winthrops were a nonconforming family who practiced their Puritanism within the church, and when young Squire John turned fourteen they sent him to Trinity College, Cambridge, reputed to be "a hotbed of Puritanism."

John later described himself as "a wild and dissolute lad," which seems to mean nothing worse than that he liked good food and drink and enjoyed such innocent country sports as hunting. But he found student life sinful and ungodly and, furthermore, a waste of time. While at Trinity and "lying abed of an illness," he first drew near to God, but not until much later and after years of soul-searching did he satisfy himself that he had indeed experienced true conversion.

Leaving Cambridge at sixteen he returned to Groton, married Mary Forth, a neighboring heiress, and entered on the duties of his heritage. These included managing the farm profitably, supervising its ordinary tasks such as plowing, reaping, and threshing, and seeing that the men and maidservants performed their chores. It meant also that John would take his place in the political and social life of the country and consort with neighboring Puritan squires who viewed the state of English society with pessimism and alarm. In 1613 he went to London and studied law for a time at Gray's Inn, then returned to become a justice of the peace, preside over local courts, and sit on the bench with his fellow magistrates at more important sessions. It was a good life and a challenging one, and developed the young man's administrative ability, which he was to use well when he came to rule over Massachusetts Bay.

The diary he kept—like Bradford's, a fine historical source—is full of his spiritual struggles, long periods of prayer and wrestling with the worldly side of his nature. Passionate in his attempts to seek communion with God and to cleanse his soul of its impurities, he developed a deep sincerity of purpose and an integrity of life. When he felt in harmony with God and God's universe, he thrilled to eager joy. When he perceived flaws and weaknesses in himself he sought stubbornly to correct them. If he spent much of his time in disciplining other people, he was able to do it with skill and honesty because he had first disciplined himself.

Every moment that he could spare from his necessary duties he tried to devote to God, praying aloud and singing hymns as he rode his horse to London. How to live in the world of wickedness and lust and luxury and still maintain the essential virtues Puritanism demanded was the lifelong problem of John Winthrop, and he never ceased trying to solve it.

His first wife died in 1615 leaving several children, and the widower soon married Thomasine Clopton, who did not long survive. In April, 1618, a third bride came home to Groton Manor, Margaret, daughter of Sir John Tyndal of Great Maplestead in Essex. Margaret was the true love of John Winthrop's life, and their long and happy marriage ended only with her death a little before his own. During their early years he had to be absent from her much of the time, and their letters are full of the understanding and love between them. Written with dignity and restraint, they revealed the ardent and romantic passion they felt for each other. Some of the Puritans may have been bleak and chilly lovers, but not this pair.

During the 1620's Winthrop began to feel for the first time the need of more money. A country gentleman in modest circumstances had nevertheless a social position to maintain and many calls upon his purse. Luxurious living prevailed, and it cost a man more and more every year to send his children forth into the world. Depression hit the cloth trade, and the eastern shires, where many Puritans dwelt, suffered heavily from it. Wool went unsold, looms grew silent, and families were hungry. To solve his personal situation, Winthrop developed a legal practice in London and served as an attorney for His Majesty's Court of Wards and Liveries. He and Margaret discussed moving their family to town, but they never did so, preferring instead the green fields and villages of their native countryside.

Meanwhile King Charles and his religious adviser, Bishop Laud, began to make conditions steadily more difficult for Nonconformists. In March, 1629, the King dismissed his Puritan Parliament and henceforth governed without it, making all men subject directly to the royal will. Winthrop lost his government position, and persecution increased on every hand. Nonconformist ministers were silenced, thrown out of their livings, even imprisoned. People began to talk darkly of the old days when Bloody Mary ordered the Protestant martyrs burned at Smithfield, and wondered if those days would come back.

John Winthrop wrote to his wife, "I am verily persuaded, God will bring some heavye Affliction upon this land, and that speedylye; but be of good comfort . . . if the Lord seeth it will be good for us, he will provide a shelter and a hidinge place. . . ."

For the next few months Winthrop busied himself writing letters and documents supporting the cause of Nonconformity—religious reformation of the Anglican church from within —and these circulated freely among those who thought as he did, increasing his reputation for wisdom, godliness, and leadership. In July he rode north with his brother-in-law, Emmanuel Downing, swearing mildly, perhaps, when his horse tumbled him into a fen, but taking it as no ill omen.

Tattershall in Lincolnshire, home of Isaac Johnson and his

wife, the Lady Arbella, was an ancient house, built before the Wars of the Roses. Stalwart brickwork made it one of the best fortified seats in England. But the future, not the past, held possession of it that summer, as its rafters echoed with the comings and goings of the men who would soon make history in a new land. Simon Bradstreet, engaged to marry Anne, daughter of Thomas Dudley and America's first poetess; Dudley himself, doughty and obstinate; John Cotton, Thomas Leverett, Richard Bellingham, Saltonstalls, Eliots, young Roger Williams, whom nobody knew quite what to do with— they were all in and out or sent messages there.

The group had worked together to form a joint company for settling land round Massachusetts Bay, and they had a charter from the King. Best of all, the charter did not specify where the group must maintain its headquarters and center of government, though the royal intent had been undoubtedly to keep it in London. But these daring Nonconformists had determined to send a group across the sea, carrying the charter with them and establishing its authority beyond the interference of the King. Who could better lead them than John Winthrop, they insisted, when he visited them that summer. He had his own doubts at first, fewer doubts when he discussed it later with his friends in Cambridge. By October he allowed himself to be elected as their governor for the coming year, and began to make arrangements for the passage westward.

From all England they came, the men who would help John Winthrop found his Nonconformist paradise in America. West country folk sailed out of Plymouth and Bristol; those from London and the eastern shires, including the governor himself and his three sons, embarked at Southampton.

It was the beginning of the great Puritan migration that would flow westward until the beginning of the civil war some twelve years later. The tiny *Mayflower* had set out in the late summer, poorly provisioned, poor in everything but spirit, at the financial mercy of the penny-pinching merchants in London. But the *Arbella* that bore John Winthrop was a stout ship, well stocked, well-manned, and well-equipped with guns. In a leather case rode the charter, instrument of power, and close behind followed the *Talbot,* the *Ambrose,* and the *Jewel.* Nearly seven hundred people sailed with Winthrop, two hundred joined him shortly after he reached Salem, and on their heels came a thousand more.

After a voyage troubled by threats of violence that never materialized, they landed in balmy June weather, 1630, and were welcomed by the earlier settlers who had taken up land within their patent. The gentry supped on venison pasty and beer, and the others hastened eagerly ashore to pick wild strawberries, reputed to be larger and sweeter than we find them today and delicious after weeks of ship's diet. Amply supplied with food for the time being and sure of a long summer ahead, the Winthrop company could start to explore the land and set up their government.

After considering several sites they decided to build their town on the peninsula of Shawmut or Trimontaine, and by September 7 they had agreed to call it Boston after the old English town, home to so many of them. Springs of sweet water flowed from its hillsides, and fertile islands lay in the bay before it. It would be an easy site to defend. It had a good harbor for ships. They began to put up frame houses, a church, and fortifications. They set aside a common.

Winthrop was already meeting with his assistants provided

for in the charter and was beginning to work out a government "in no ways repugnant to the known laws of England"
and still in keeping with the ideal of what a Puritan commonwealth ought to be.

From here on, as with Bradford, we must neglect the full
story of the colony if we are to tell the story of the man.

Winthrop enjoyed a happy family life for most of the nineteen years he lived in Massachusetts, but his days were not
without tragedy. His son Henry drowned soon after his arrival, and a daughter died at sea while Margaret was bringing
the rest of the family to him in 1631. Always a devoted public
servant, he impoverished his own estate repeatedly to further
the common good and spent his last days in somewhat strait-
ened circumstances, aided by his son John. For nine years he
served as governor, and for ten years as deputy governor or
assistant, never being entirely out of office. He first lost the
governorship in 1634 when he was replaced by Thomas Dudley. He had failed to be reelected through no fault of his own.
Reverend John Cotton had arrived the preceding September
and preached the strange doctrine that magistrates must con-
tinue in office until they proved themselves to be unfit. The
rank and file of Massachusetts voters felt that they had to show
him the power of free election still lay in their hands.

Throughout the entire period Winthrop found himself
faced with a rising tide of democracy which he could not
check, particularly as the back country opened up and men
could move about freely, acquiring new land. Although
founded on the laws of the Old Testament, Winthrop's government as he administered it was neither harsh nor unjust.
But he did believe that the people should be governed and
not govern, that a magistrate once elected had sole power. It

may seem autocratic to us, but the Englishmen of that day had never been used to any government that was not autocratic. Nor can we completely understand the intermingling of church and civil authority which prevailed in the Bay Colony. Perhaps only Roger Williams, whom we shall meet later, ever saw it clearly.

Dudley found John Winthrop too mild, soft, and lenient. Often reproved for these traits, John grew harsher and more narrow with advancing years. During these decades, too, the church encroached more and more upon secular matters. Winthrop never took a strong stand against this and consulted frequently with the clergy; an astute politician, he was capable of getting his own way by devious—but never dishonest—methods. Too austere, perhaps, to be truly loved, he never lost the loyalty of his people. When Anne Hutchinson was banished from the colony for stirring up heresy, he sided firmly against her, seeing her rebellion as a threat to political as well as religious order.

In 1639 he successfully defended the charter when attacks were made upon it in England; and he won reelection in that year, though the ministers, never too friendly to his purely civil rule, were working against him, telling folk that he sought to hold the office for life. While Winthrop did believe that the freemen—church members only—had a right to vote, he disliked legislation and preferred to govern under the loose provisions of the charter. When Nathaniel Ward finally wrote down and codified the law, as it was practiced in Massachusetts, into a document called "The Body of Liberties," Winthrop acknowledged it without enthusiasm.

The year 1643 proved eventful for the former owner of Groton Manor. It saw the forming of the United Colonies of

New England, a project that had been dear to him for some years. This was based on an agreement entered into by Massachusetts, Plymouth, Connecticut, and New Haven Colonies, pledging them to come to one another's aide in case of Indian attack and establishing their various contributions of troops and money. Winthrop was one of the chief architects of the plan and its first president. It did not overly disturb him that the other colonies were beginning to grumble against the arrogance and encroachment of the Bay.

Another event proved less happy. One bright June day he and Margaret and three of their young sons took a pleasure jaunt to an island in the Bay known as "the Governor's Garden." While they were enjoying the cool salt air and the play of sunlight on the blue waves, an excited woman beached her small boat and ran toward them. A French ship had just passed the fort, she panted, an armed ship, the first one ever to threaten the safety of Boston. Before Winthrop could take any action a shallop swiftly approached the Governor's Garden and a party of uniformed Frenchmen swarmed ashore. At their head he recognized La Tour, one of the two rivals for the governorship of Arcadia. La Tour and his opponent, D'Aulnay, had both received the assignment from the ministers of Louis XIII, and were carrying out their quarrel among the fishing villages of the northeast coast. La Tour had not come here in hostility, he hastily told the governor, only to seek aid against his enemy.

Winthrop considered the situation. It was to his interests to keep the quarrel alive so that neither of the Frenchmen could grow strong enough to attack the Bay. Moreover, La Tour seemed to him to be the weaker, and therefore the better one to help. He finally allowed the French to land and stay in town for a time where they might try to enlist help from private sources. They did win some support, although there was much muttering in the streets of Boston about their presence there. Once when the vividly clad strangers drilled on Boston Common it seemed that a riot might break out, but they eventually sailed away without bloodshed. The measure had been so unpopular, however, that the next year Winthrop failed to be reelected.

Chosen again in 1645, he held the office until his death. Critics and agitators troubled his remaining years, but he stood up stoutly against them. He lost his beloved Margaret in 1647 and took a fourth wife, Martha Coytmore.

Winthrop died on March 26, 1649, worn out with grief, self-sacrifice, and hard work. Some of his earlier kindliness and mercy returned as he lay on his deathbed. When a delegation came to him and asked that he sign an order for banishment, he refused, saying that he had done too much of that work already.

A good governor he was, if we accept the ideal of what he thought his mission to be—that he and his fellow magistrates were divinely commissioned by God to establish a government of the Gospel in a new colony. And if he made little contribution to democratic political theory, at least he gave the Bay a strong government that held its people together and enabled it to grow into the future state. A noble and sensitive spirit, he lacked the simple common sense of Bradford, and he could rejoice with some maliciousness over misfortunes which befell those whom he considered enemies of God. Like all of us he had his faults, but whatever talents and virtues he possessed he expended freely in the interests of those over whom he ruled.

"A worthy gentleman," wrote one historian, "who has done good in Israel, having spent not only his whole estate . . . but his bodily strength and life in the service of the country; not sparing, but always as the burning torch, spending.

Chapter 2

‧‧‧‧‧‧‧ ∞ ‧‧‧‧‧‧‧

ROGER WILLIAMS

One summer day in 1629 three young clergymen sat in a tavern under the shadow of St. Botolph's great square tower known as "Boston Stump" and looked out at the pink brick houses of the old seaport town of Boston in Lincolnshire. They looked past the houses to the ships in the river that swung at their moorings as if eager to be gone. The young men talked of the evil days that had fallen on England and the cause of the Puritans there. They shook their heads above their wine and goose pasty and looked over their shoulders now and then to see if one of Bishop Laud's spies could be anywhere about. They talked of the group that called itself the Massachusetts Bay Company now forming at Isaac Johnson's manor in Sempringham, and they wondered if perhaps it might be better for them to join this company and sail beyond the sea.

The men were John Cotton of Boston, Thomas Hooker of Chelmsford, and Roger Williams, chaplain to Sir William Masham at his country estate in Essex. All of them did eventually go to America and make names for themselves there. But no name in early American history shines brighter today than

that of Roger Williams; and if the men of his own time referred to him as "divinely mad" and "having windmills in
his head," he seems to us the sanest of all his contemporaries,
the easiest for us to understand. Bradford and Winthrop
maintained friendly relations with him, but his presence always made them uneasy, for they did not share his ideals or
sympathize with his dream. Paul Revere and the patriots of
the Revolution would have understood him better. And we
who have enjoyed all our lives the religious liberty he fought
for find it hard to imagine a time when such liberty was not
the birthright of every American. It is largely due to Roger
Williams that we have this inherent right, but in establishing
it he had to come a hard and thorny way.

A London lad from birth, he grew up in the rich, squalid,
medieval city; the Tower, London Bridge, Billingsgate fish-
market, the shops of Cheapside, and the broad "Walk" of St.
Paul's were as familiar to him as the Yorkshire lanes were to
William Bradford. The Great Fire destroyed St. Sepulchre
with the record of his birth, which probably took place in
1603. His father, James Williams, was a member of the Merchant Taylor's Guild and kept a shop located at the front of
his dwelling house in Cow Lane on Snow Hill just outside
London Wall. Across the street stood a tavern called the Har-
row owned by James's wife, Alice Pemberton Williams. She
came of a wealthier stock than her husband, a landed family
in Hertfordshire. Many of her kin were prominent, and one,
Sir James Pemberton, became Lord Mayor of London the
year Roger was ten years old.

Snow Hill, a steep crooked thoroughfare thronged with
coaches, wagons, and foot travelers, wound through a new
and fashionable part of the city, but not so fashionable as to

exclude trade. A printer, an ironmonger, and a scrivener had shops nearby. Only a little way off lay Smithfield, an open space of some five acres that had long been the playground of the city. Men watered their beasts at its shallow pond when they came to the horse fair or the haymarket. Almost every day some sort of sale went on here, and Roger could race with the other boys of the neighborhood past pens holding pigs, cows, and oxen, past booths displaying farm implements, country produce, and all sorts of peasant ware. The Cloth Fair was held here too, on St. Bartholomew's Day. Roger's father took a prominent part; the Lord Mayor came, and the sheriffs in their violet gowns; the scarlet and gold coats of the nobility flashed here and there among the leather jerkins and drab jackets of humbler folk. Puppet shows, magicians, fortunetellers, peddlers of all kinds of knickknacks and sweetmeats, tempted the people to spend their pennies. The Williams children—three brothers and sister Katherine— could not have been strangers to these revels of merrie England.

Sometimes they went to see water pageants on the Thames or watched royal processions passing toward Westminster. Sometimes Roger stood outside nearby Newgate Prison and scanned its dreary walls, his heart full of pity and anger as he thought of the men inside it whose political and religious opinions had angered the King. As a child he became—he left us no record of how—an ardent Puritan, for which, he wrote later, he was "persecuted in and out of my father's house." No doubt the family upbraided him and tried to keep him from joining the rebellious sect, but he was neither cast out nor disinherited.

A bright lad, quick to learn, he picked up some skill in

what passed for shorthand in that day, and drew the attention of Sir Edward Coke, the great Puritan lawyer who was chief authority on English common law. Coke let him record the proceedings of the Court of the Star Chamber and sponsored him at Charter House School, which he attended on scholarship. James Williams died in the autumn of 1621, leaving Alice to administer the family fortunes, and two years later Roger entered Pembroke Hall at Cambridge. Here he turned his back on cockfights, boxing matches, or trips to Sturbridge Fair, to consort with other Puritan scholars, of whom he found many. After taking his degree in 1627 he stayed on for further study until Laud's zealous persecution began to reach even into study and lecture hall. February, 1629, found young Mr. Williams installed as chaplain at Oates, a fine estate in the rich farmlands of Essex that belonged to the Puritan gentleman Sir William Masham.

To Sir William's home came all the important Puritan leaders of the time; the Earls of Bedford, Lincoln, and Warwick, Sir Oliver St. Johns, Sir Henry Martin, Sir Arthur Haselrig, Sir Richard Saltonstall, and Oliver Cromwell. Seated familiarly with them at table and in the drawing room, the young chaplain made friendships that would prove helpful to him in later years when he came back from New England to seek aid and protection for his colony. But sometimes as the spring weather grew softer and warmer he felt restless in the sober company of the men and slipped away from them. The Essex fields turned white with daisies and the hedgerows white with hawthorn, birds sang in the copses, and lovers strolled the lanes by moonlight. Roger Williams strolled with Jane Whalley, daughter of a noble Puritan family, sister of Sir Edward, who would later sign King Charles's death warrant and in turn have to flee for his own life.

Jane and Roger were in love, that spring of 1629, and wanted to marry, but Jane's aunt, Lady Joan Barrington, in whose care she was living, refused the suit of the penniless young cleric; not quite penniless, perhaps, but his "little yet costly study of books and prospects of twenty pounds a year" did not impress Lady Joan as promising much of a future for her niece. She and Roger exchanged sharp letters that ended the affair. Alice Williams in London had not approved of it either. Roger fell into a burning fever but recovered, and soon found another girl to stroll with in the lanes. Mary Barnard, maid to Lady Masham's daughter, had no dragons to guard her. Her hand was her own to give, and she bestowed it where she would. By the time the great hall at Oates turned festive with Christmas holly she had married Roger Williams and begun to share his reluctant dreams of a new land.

Not much is known about Mary save that she made him a good wife through all the hardships of pioneer living, able to administer his home and his business affairs whenever he had to leave them in her care. That she was "a maid" does not necessarily mean that she was an unlettered servant. Well-born young girls often took service in the homes of family friends, in both old and New England. She may have been the daughter of a parson in Nottingham, according to some evidence. Her husband's letters prove that they shared a tender companionship, and it is doubtful if he long regretted the lost Jane.

But love affairs never distracted Roger Williams from his religious devotion, always the prime concern of his life. Although he liked the Puritan ways as a young child, he did not withdraw from the Anglican church and remained in membership during his student days. When he rode north with Hooker and Cotton he discussed with them his ideas which had become more and more like those of the Separatists. He could no longer, he felt, hold with the Book of Common Prayer, the formal services, and Laud's church reform. Hooker and Cotton shook their heads, unwilling to go quite that far.

Bishop and King grew increasingly more tyrannical. On all sides the young Puritan saw men of his opinions face loss of living, whippings, torture, and imprisonment. He did not want to leave the country he loved, but he knew that he could not stay there in safety and worship according to his conscience. With Mary he fled to Bristol where they met young John Winthrop, and the two spoke darkly of their future at home, hopefully of Massachusetts Bay. "It was bitter as death to me when Bishop Laud pursued me out of this land," Williams later wrote. Unwillingly he boarded the ship *Lyon* one winter day and sailed westward over a storm-tossed sea.

After a rough voyage of sixty-seven days the *Lyon* entered ice-choked Boston Harbor in early February, 1631. The colony at first welcomed the newcomer as a godly and zealous man and gave him a call to their church, which he refused to accept when he found they were "an unseparated people." This shocked and angered them. Furthermore, he insisted on soul liberty and a separation of church and state, denying that the magistrates could punish anyone for religious offenses such as blasphemy, heresy, and idolatry. Boston shook from the waterside to the summit of Beacon Hill.

Worse followed in April when the Salem church called Mr. Williams to be its teacher. Believing it to be more Separatist than it actually was, he accepted the call but later withdrew to Plymouth. His long quarrel with the Boston theocrats had begun, though Winthrop remained his friend.

At Plymouth he held no office, but preached, prayed, and became a church member and a free man of the colony. Granted a house and land, he learned for the first time to hoe corn, tend farm animals, and till the soil. He learned, too, the value of Indian friendships, and began to establish a profitable trade with them, sat in their smoky wigwams, and brought them the word of God.

Plymouth made him welcome but never joined him in his insistence on complete religious liberty, complete separation from the English church. Bradford wrote thus of him after he had returned to Salem to embroil himself in further controversy:

> A man godly and zealous, having many precious parts, but very unsettled in judgment . . . this year he began to fall into some strange opinions and from opinions to practice which caused some controversy between the church and him. He is to be pitied and prayed for, and so I leave the matter, and desire the Lord to show him his errors and reduce him into the way of truth and give him a settled judgment and constancy in the same.

Roger Williams arrived in Salem in the summer of 1633 and lived there, preaching in the church and ministering to the people for the next two years, though harassed constantly by the establishment at Boston. As his opinions became more and more pronounced and gained increasing support, the leaders of the Bay ranged themselves solidly against him. He threatened not only the validity of their religious beliefs but the very foundations of their power. He was a dangerous rebel and they moved against him, slowly but with no uncertainty as to the final outcome. Roger Williams must recant or go.

Added to his Separatist views were further declarations, which angered many and disturbed even fair-minded Winthrop. He refused to take their oaths of loyalty, defended liberty of conscience for all, and denied that the magistrates could punish for religious offenses. He protested against taxation for church support and the maintenance of a "hireling ministry." Let the preachers live by the sweat of their brows as other men did, as he did himself. The Word of God was not to be sold for pay. And perhaps most outrageously of all, he argued that the Massachusetts settlers had no right to their lands unless they had purchased them from the Indians.

Summoned to answer for his errors, he refused to recant. After several hearings and much petty squabbling over such points as whether women should wear veils and the symbolic use of the cross—which Williams favored—he received sentence of banishment in October, 1635. All the great men of Massachusetts met at Newtown for Williams's arraignment: Governor Haynes, Richard Bellingham, Thomas Dudley, William Coddington, Simon Bradstreet, and his erstwhile friends Cotton and Hooker. They affirmed their position: "In the religious and civil affairs the church was to be the highest authority. The Bible was the source of all law and justice. The state was merely the civil arm to carry out her decrees and penalties." Roger Williams could never subscribe to these principles. He retired to Salem, determined to keep on waging the war though he had lost the battle.

Fortunately he was granted permission to remain until

spring. His wife had just borne a second daughter, and his own health failed him, but he continued to hold private meetings in his house to preach to those who would listen. He had withdrawn from the Salem church when it refused to separate from Anglicanism; but Mary still attended it, and he did not interfere with her right of free worship. Many Salem folk still loved him and went to his meetings, particularly the women. A handsome man, courteous and polished, with all the sophistication of the university and the great country houses, he always drew a large feminine audience wherever he went. But alas, the goodwives of Salem could not save him.

Angered at his unshaken popularity, at the threat he must be to them so long as he remained within their borders, the court met in January and ordered him to be taken at once to England. Winthrop sent him a warning of their intent, with the advice that he flee in all haste to the Narragansett country. Williams already owned land which he had received in an exchange of gifts with the Indians. All in one winter afternoon he arranged his affairs and set out in the teeth of a driving blizzard.

And this is how history has delighted to picture him, striding against the snowstorm, plodding through frozen swamps and icy thickets, one man alone, behind him all the entrenched bigotry, the stern rock-bound coasts of New England Puritanism, before him the fertile acres of Narragansett where he would establish religious freedom and political democracy, the America of the future.

After a terrible journey of fourteen weeks across "a howling wilderness of frost and snow, not knowing what bed or bread could mean," Williams arrived at the Indian village of Sowams in the Narragansett country. Its chiefs, Canonicus and Miantonomo, had entered into a dispute with Massasoit, and Williams helped to settle it, thus winning their favor, hospitality, and grants of land. A sincere friend to the tribesmen, he understood their language and he always treated them with kindness and justice. He had built up a thriving Indian trade from his first days in New England, and the chiefs often granted him land in return for gifts or services. He never tried to convert them by force, but went frequently among their wigwams, ministering to the sick, praying and preaching whenever they would listen. He walked warily, however, seeing them as "wolves endowed with men's brains," whose goodwill could never be wholly depended upon.

That spring of 1636 he began a settlement on the east bank of the Seekonk River, taking with him William Harris, "poor and destitute"; John Smith, a miller banished from Dorchester; Francis Wickes, "a poor fellow"; and "a lad of Richard Waterman's." Shortly afterward Plymouth Colony protested that this land lay within their patent, and he arranged to remove westward to an area of Narragansett Bay which still bears the name he gave it—Providence.

When Roger Williams and his poor following paddled up the Great Salt River in May, 1636, they stepped ashore on a peninsula with a spring of sweet water and a high hill from whence they could view the surrounding countryside. Oaks and cedars covered it. Ancient forests stretched away to the east, and swamps of coarse salt grass spread westward. To the north lay barrens of scrubby pine and the rock and granite ridges of the back country. Williams built his own house close to the spring on a shallow stone foundation with hewn timbers rising above. Larger than most of the two-room homes constructed by the other men on the ten-acre lots along

Towne Street, it served for years as the center of colony life.
Here Indians came, town meetings assembled, and refugees
flocked during the Pequot War. Food supplies never lacked,
for corn lands abounded, clam and oyster beds lay along the
shores, wild deer, moose, and fowl dwelt in the nearby woods.
Mary and the children soon joined him and accustomed
themselves to the rough-hewn chests and stools, the iron pots
and wooden spoons, the scarceness of comfort and luxury. It
was not so different from Salem, but it was certainly unlike
the English manors or the gabled, close-set houses of London.

Williams kept the principal powers in his own hands for
the first two years, but from the very beginning the heads of
families gathered to consult on all affairs of the colony and
agreed to be governed by the demands of the common good—
except in matters of religion, where every man was free. Un-
derlying the administration of Providence was a recognition
of the natural rights of man, the consent of individuals to a
social compact establishing government, and complete freedom of worship. More men soon came to join in the experiment, and Providence grew rapidly. Some were refugees from
Massachusetts or free thinkers from overseas; others were only
poor folk seeking subsistence. Roger Williams made a place
for all of them.

He sold land so cheaply that men could easily become property holders and thereby qualified to vote. He bought islands
in Narragansett Bay, and other settlers established the towns
of Portsmouth and Newport on what he first called "the Island of Rhode Island." Through his good offices the bloody
Pequot War came to an end favorable to the Narragansetts
and the white men. There is a saying that not everybody will
be pleased with Paradise, and certainly everybody was not

pleased with Providence Plantations. Disputes arose among the citizens. Some resented the leadership of Williams. The men of the Bay considered his followers as outlaws and excommunicates. They would not trade with these heretics or allow them to travel to Boston, and they threatened to destroy what they called "this sink of iniquity which hath every shade of opinion except Catholics and true Christians." In 1643 the three towns of the Narragansett commissioned Williams to go to England and seek a charter which would give them the legal foundation they needed. He sold some of his island property to finance the trip and sailed from New York, as he was unwelcome at the port of Boston.

The England that Roger Williams returned to was not the England he had left twelve years before. The Thames still flowed under London Bridge, and farmers still brought their wares to Smithfield Market as they had done for centuries, but new men were in power and new ideas raised a clamor on every side. Civil war had broken out, and armies trampled the cornfields of the quiet shires. Bishop Laud lay a prisoner in the Tower. King Charles had fled to Oxford, and Parliament governed without him. Changes, too, had come about in the Williams family. Alice Williams had died in 1635 and left a legacy to her son which he was never able to claim because he would not swear an oath to court testimony.

On his arrival Williams went at once to the home of his old friend Sir Harry Vane and then took lodgings of his own in the heart of the city, as eagerly active here as he had been on the shores of Narragansett Bay. A powerful group called the "Independents" had risen, led by a number of Williams's friends, and he joined it at once, since they believed in his ideals of religious toleration and civil liberty. All that winter he went about preaching and writing in support of his views, journeying into the country sometimes to arrange for the delivery of firewood to poor London families whose supply was cut off by the war. He visited with the poet Milton, also with Cromwell, Haselrig, Barrington, and Sir William Masham, his old patron—all prominent Independents. These men held power and they used it in his behalf. Massachusetts, too, had sent representatives to try to obtain a patent for the Narragansett land, but Williams held the greater influence and got his claim recognized with little difficulty. Before he sailed for home in the summer of 1644 he had made a reputation for achievements other than the charter.

Politics never tempted him from religion, and after listening to the church services of the many sects that had settled in Providence, he had evolved a creed of his own—a further development of his original Separatism. Now he began to preach this creed in London, and it won many followers. They were called "Seekers," because Williams had come to believe that no church on earth held any real spiritual authority and that the only way to find God was to seek him through solitary prayer and meditation. Virtue he believed in, but not austerity, and his faith had a natural mysticism, a richness and warmth that drew men to follow him. His striking appearance had a part in it, too; his sharp bold jaw contrasted with deep, soft eyes. In vain did his critics cry out that he was "sowing seed which sprouts in wild and bitter fruit." Many of the leading Independents joined this group or meditated on its teachings, which led them to a greater sympathy for the oppressed souls and bodies of men.

Roger Williams's English visit also resulted in the publication of his two major books. The first of these, *A Key Into the*

Language of America, he worked on during the voyage, and it began by being a phrase book of several Indian dialects, chiefly Narragansett, and ended as a treasurehouse of knowledge about Indian tongues, folklore, customs, and religion. His second book, *The Bloody Tenet of Persecution,* was more controversial and did not appear until its author was safely on his way back to America. It described his quarrel with the Boston Puritans, and the free society founded on the rights of man which he had erected at Providence. It emphasized the separation of church and state, the right of every man to worship as he chose and not be forced to support and give lip service to any other form of worship. It spoke out so forcefully against religious persecution that even today it remains a living and vital document, one of the cornerstones of our American liberties. Some of his critics spoke of him as "trumpeting rebellion." Others succeeded in having copies of his book burned by the common hangman. A flood of pamphlets burst forth attacking it. But its ideas had laid a strong hold on men's minds and played an important part in the political philosophy that would triumph with the execution of King Charles at the end of the Civil War.

When Roger Williams landed in Boston with his charter for Providence Plantations, he brought also letters from members of Parliament to the authorities at the Bay, recommending that he be given hospitable welcome and allowed to proceed unmolested through their territory. This permission they yielded but grudgingly, saying that they had not changed their opinion of Williams and were of no mind to grant him further favors. His own people welcomed him with great enthusiasm, however, and meetings were at once called to work out a code of laws for governing the colony. These meetings went on for several years and were gatherings of the people rather than assemblies of delegates. Nor did the business run smoothly, for Narragansett folk distrusted centralized authority. Furthermore they were of such varied religious beliefs that mutual understanding and agreement proved difficult. Squabbles and petty jealousies arose between towns and individuals.

They did manage to establish a government with executive, legislative, and judicial branches, and chose Williams as their first "chief officer." Much of his time had to be spent at the trading post which supported his family, and he gave much attention to Indian affairs, keeping up his missionary work and acting as peacemaker when the other colonies were threatened. Although he was only in middle age, his hair had turned white and his health began to break, but he did not spare himself in striving to make his colony the secure haven of free men that he had envisioned it to be.

Always the Bay schemed to encroach on his patent, and in 1651 William Coddington of Newport, richest man in the colony, received a grant of the Island of Rhode Island with the provision that he should be its governor for life. This was within Williams's patent, and his people arose to defend his earlier and better established claim. Once again the former London lad found it necessary to cross the sea.

He remained in England until the spring of 1654. He saw Cromwell set up his protectorate and attempt to govern without Parliament, a thing Williams could not approve of. The Seekers now numbered many thousand all over England and Wales, and he visited with some of these groups, giving them encouragement and fresh inspiration. But he found time to read Dutch with Milton, Cromwell's Latin secretary, miserable in the first stages of his blindness. Many of the old Independents were falling from power, but their influence remained strong enough to get Coddington's patent set aside and Williams's original claims restored.

This time he did not receive a glorious welcome home. Two parties were forming in the colony, beginning a struggle that would go on for years; and quarrels, accusations, and petty intrigues plagued Providence Plantations. Against Williams's law and order party, the followers of William Harris tried to set up a condition of complete anarchy, under which men should be subject to no laws whatsoever. Harris was tried, convicted of treason, and put on good behavior. Never during the remaining years of Williams's life did the anarchists gain control, but his enemies harassed him until he could say, "Since I set the first step of any English foot into these wild parts . . . what have I reaped of the root of being the stepping stone of so many families and towns about us, but grief, sorrow and bitterness?"

Two new and important groups of immigrants came to Providence Plantations during the few years after the return of Williams from England. In 1656 came the Quakers, persecuted at the Bay and unwelcome at Plymouth. And from New York and the West Indies arrived several small parties of Jews to set up their famous community at Newport, which was to provide the most happy experience this people enjoyed in early America. Williams welcomed both groups, although he disapproved of the Quaker doctrine and disorderly behavior.

Changes in England always threatened change in America, and with the restoration of the Stuarts in 1660, Williams feared that the new King might frown upon the party that had beheaded his father. And frown upon them he did, but Providence was not included in the royal displeasure. Instead it received a new charter in 1663 for a free and absolute civil government under the name of Rhode Island. This allowed the colony to retain its democracy, defined the boundaries, and gave the people the right to travel and trade in other colonies. Roger Williams was appointed one of the ten assistants to serve until the next election, and he began at once to set up the new state, incorporating all that had been good in the old. Still plagued with petty dissensions and the machinations of William Harris, but aided by his long-time associate, Benedict Arnold, he continued for the rest of his life, in one elective office or another, to serve his colony.

In 1672 George Fox visited the Quakers of Rhode Island, "a wild, coarse fanatic in leather breeches," to encourage his followers in their obstreperous behavior. He referred to Williams as "the New England Firebrand" and "a wild Ishmael whose hand is against every man." Williams challenged him to a public debate, but Fox did not stay for it. Later several of his followers agreed to debate with Williams, who wrote, "And God graciously assisted me in rowing all day with my old bones so that I got to Newport toward midnight before the morning appointed." The mighty argument went on for three days and was later continued at Providence. It confined itself largely to Quaker doctrine rather than any indictment of individuals, and Williams asserted that he loved and honored many of that persuasion. Nothing was settled, though vast crowds gathered to hear the speakers, and two books appeared afterward, each giving the author's point of view. Williams produced *George Fox Digg'd Out Of His Burrow* almost immediately, and Fox answered it with *The New England Firebrand Quenched,* some five years later.

The dispute with the Quakers was followed by the bloody outrage of King Philip's War, when a young, headstrong chief made a last desperate attempt to oust the white man. Rhode Island did not join the United Colonies in pursuing it, but they armed themselves to protect their homes, and Roger Williams served as a captain in the Providence Trainband. Having done all he could to avoid bloodshed by counseling moderation on both sides, he had to watch the refugees from the back country fleeing to the safety of the islands. After the unmerciful slaughter of the Great Swamp Fight, the remaining Indians retaliated by burning Providence, except for twenty houses including Williams's own. In the wake of the colonists' inevitable victory, he tried to help both whites and Indians who had suffered from the war.

Roger Williams spent his last years working on his manuscripts, preaching to his people, faithfully discharging whatever civil duties he was called to. A devoted Seeker to the end, he constantly sought for "the unsearchable mind and mystery of God," through the study of Holy Writ and the endeavors of his own spirit. A friend to the creative arts, his religion found a place for them, unusual in that day. Music, painting, and poetry, even embroidery and decoration, he felt, could play their part in the worship of the God who had inspired them.

Still mentally alert, he and Mary enjoyed an old age blessed with the goodness of their children. "Can you find such another now alive or in this age," his son Daniel wrote of him later. "He gave away his lands and other estates to them that he thought were most in want, until he gave away all, so that he had nothing to help himself; so that he, not being in a way to get for his supply, and being ancient, it needs must pinch somewhere. I do not say what I have done for both father and mother: I judge that they want nothing that is convenient for ancient people." This has been interpreted to mean that Williams died a pauper, but records show him to have been land poor.

The date of his death is as unknown to us as that of his birth, but it occurred early in 1683. His neighbors gathered to hear the Trainband fire a volley over his grave in the frozen hillside and to comfort Mary. More ideas that have become national, according to the historian Bancroft, have emanated from the little colony of Rhode Island than from any other. The Plymouth men preceded him, but he carried the ideals of toleration and democracy beyond their beginnings at Plymouth. He could hoe corn, drive a shrewd bargain in the fur trade, or devise a new religious doctrine. He was as at home in the smoky wigwams of the Indians as in the political circles of London. He could erect a modern state in the wilderness. But he was first of all a man of the spirit who could write:

Alas, Sir, in the calm midnight thoughts, what are these leaves and flowers and smoke and shadows of earthly things, about which we poor fools and children disquiet ourselves in vain? . . . What are all the contentions and wars of the world about, generally, but for greater dishes and bowls of porridge? . . . All these are but sublunaries, temporaries and trivials. Eternity, O Eternity is our business.

Your long despised Outcast,

Roger Williams

Chapter 3

———⟨∞⟩———

COTTON MATHER

A generation ago when the poems of John Greenleaf Whittier were household words, his readers received their first introduction to the Puritan minister Cotton Mather. "The Double-headed Snake of Newbury" was a poem that sent delicious shivers coursing up young spines and caused their elders to give uneasy shrugs and cast backward glances over the shoulder. This snake, a seventeenth-century apparition that infested the Newbury marshes, had a head at either end of its long, coiling body, according to local report. It seems to have aroused a good deal of terror. Perhaps it had come from the Devil himself on a Satanic mission. Perhaps it was the same undying serpent that tempted Eve. Anyhow, the leading minds of early Massachusetts, ministers and laymen alike, felt duty-bound to investigate it, and so:

> Cotton Mather came galloping down,
> All the way to Newbury town,
> With his eyes agog and his ears set wide,
> And his marvelous inkhorn at his side;
> Stirring awhile in the shallow pool

47

Of his brains for the lore he learned at school,
To garnish the story with here a streak
Of Latin, and there another of Greek:
And the tales he told and the notes he took,
Behold! Are they not in his Wonder Book!

We get an unfavorable picture at once, of a sort of popeyed frogman rushing inquisitively about, a creature of little natural wit, dull and pompous and eager to parade his learning. Unfortunately the picture lingers. Whittier did not like Mather, but Whittier was a different man of a different time, a time much nearer to our own, so it is easy to accept his opinion. A passionate liberal, Whittier fought ardently for the freedom of man. Mather was not a liberal, and he found the idea of a free country "an abomination." But he fought as ardently to bring men's souls to God, which he felt was the highest service that could be performed for them. And more than that, it was a striving to perfect the harmony of the universe.

Some nine generations have lived and breathed and passed away since his friends laid Cotton Mather in the family tomb in the Copp's Hill burying ground in Boston. His life has drawn the attention of many writers. He has been so often attacked and defended that it is hard to travel backward through the maze of conflicting scholarship and try to find him as he was; harder, perhaps, to make the effort seem worthwhile. But in the belief that the effort is worthwhile, we begin with a winter day in Boston, February 12, 1663.

On that day the house of a young minister, Increase Mather, echoed with prayers of pious rejoicing. Increase and his wife, Maria, had gotten a son from the Lord. When Increase stood by the diamond-pained window of the square old house that had belonged to his father-in-law, Reverend John Cotton, of pious memory, and looked out at the streets of Boston, he wondered, perhaps, if he had made a wise choice when he returned from England nearly two years before. Son of Richard Mather, of Dorchester, one of the Bay Colony's leading ministers, he had taken his degree at Harvard College and then gone to England where he studied, preached, and made a name for himself among the dissenting congregations. But when Cromwell's Puritan commonwealth fell to pieces and the return of the Stuart kings seemed certain, young Mr. Mather decided that with this change of politics he had better try to make his career at home. Within a year he had married his stepsister, and within three years he became the minister of the Second Church of Boston, a position which he held for the rest of his life.

But he had tasted the intellectual excitement, the broader social experience, of English living, and he must sometimes have felt the limitations of this narrow colonial town. Perhaps the greatest city in America at the time, Boston contained only some seven thousand people. Its gabled houses clustered about the squares and crooked lanes of a gravelly peninsula which flood tides often cut off from the mainland. In summer cows grazed on the Common, while fruits and vegetables ripened in kitchen gardens. Great ships brought the commerce of the world to its wharves—too frequently slaves and West Indian rum, too seldom books and informative news from England. Wagons trundled over the Neck loaded with firewood, lumber, furs, and country produce from the outlying farms. But beyond these farms stretched a mysterious and threatening wilderness where wolves howled and Indians lurked, ready to bring down the unwary deer hunter with an arrow through the throat.

Whatever Increase Mather's doubts, he named his son Cotton after Reverend John, and looked on him as his boon companion, even as all his life he was boon companion to his own father. Together they would carry on the work of the Lord. Both the boy's grandfathers had preached as dissenting clergymen in England and had come to Massachusetts in the 1630's to help found and administer a true kingdom of God on earth which should be governed by the rules of scripture. In this kingdom the ministers were the ruling class, with political as well as religious authority; only church members could be free men, and only free men could vote. Nor was it easy to become a church member. Everyone must attend church, but only those who had made a profession of faith before the ministers or the congregation could be accepted as full-fledged communicants and enjoy the rights and privileges common today. Before a man could make a profession of faith he must feel the stirring of divine grace in his heart.

The Massachusetts Bay Colony followed this pattern or a gradual modification of it until late in the seventeenth century. And so young Cotton Mather, son and grandson of its leading ministers, was born into the theological aristocracy in the later days of its power. Nor was he very old before he displayed an awareness of what his heritage could mean.

Raised in an atmosphere of scholarship and pious devotion, the boy learned to pray before he learned to talk, and at eight years old he began to compose little religious exercises which he tried to get his schoolmates to repeat. Sometimes they complied good-naturedly. Sometimes they jeered and tormented

him. A frail lad, unfitted for playing wicket on the Common
or skating across the frozen ponds, he preferred to crouch
over a book by his father's fireside. Increase Mather's library
contained not only Bible commentaries and theological treatises by Latin church fathers and seventeenth-century Puritan
divines; the shelves held volumes of history, geography, medicine, mathematics, and natural science. The classics, too,
made a brave showing: Juvenal, Tacitus, Demosthenes, Hor-
ace, Plautus, Sophocles, even Ovid's *Art of Love*.

Young Cotton knew Latin at ten, and Greek and Hebrew a
few years later. At fourteen he began to discipline himself
with days of fasting and prayer. In childhood he formed the
persistent habit of examining himself constantly for evidences
of unholy vanity, wickedness, and sin—such as "whittling behind the door" on the Lord's Day. Most of the boys and girls
in colonial Boston grew up with religion as a part of their
everyday lives. They worried about sin and death and the
salvation of their souls. But they could forget it sometimes
and enjoy themselves in harmless play. Not so Cotton Mather,
who was reported to be "godly beyond all."

The fundamental beliefs of the godly in Cotton Mather's
time were derived from the religious reformer John Calvin
and ran something like this: In the beginning God created
man as a creature responsible to Him but possessing perfect
freedom of the will. When Adam sinned he used this freedom
to oppose the will of God. His sin was known as "the Fall,"
and because of it God doomed mankind to eternal punishment. A part of the punishment was that man could no longer
exercise his will in harmony with the will of God as he had
been created to do, but he was still responsible to his maker.
This state of affairs made men troubled, confused, unhappy,

ill in their minds, and prone to fall into all kinds of wickedness. Because of Christ's sacrifice on the Cross, however, God
relented somewhat and chose certain human beings who
should be absolved from punishment and assured of eternal
salvation. These were known as the "Elect." Only the Elect
should be allowed to enjoy the sweet rewards of heaven. All
other souls must end in the tormenting oblivion of eternal
fire.

Nobody, not even the wisest ministers, could tell exactly
who were of the Elect and who were not. Every man might
hope that he belonged to that fortunate company, and he
must constantly search his soul for evidences of divine grace
and mercy therein. The Elect were supposed to exert their
wills in harmony with God's. Anyone who exerted his will in
opposition remained outside God's divine harmony. Moreover, any man's slightest sin caused a great crash of discord
that echoed throughout the universe.

But how to tell the Elect from the doomed remained a
thorny question. At any moment during his life a sinner
might receive a revelation that he was to be saved. Likewise,
a good man could fall into sin. You could only pray and hope
and try to behave according to Bible standards of worthiness.
It was the duty of the ministers to encourage men to move in
accordance with divine harmony, even if their threats of hell-
fire sometimes set sensitive children to screaming in the dark.
The next world was far more important than this one. Earth
was but the antechamber to heaven—if you could get to
heaven. Death, not birth, was the supreme moment when a
man entered on his great heritage. We live but to die.

Nor did the forces of evil arise only within a man's soul. He
suffered constant threats from without. The year that Cotton

Mather entered Harvard saw the whole colony aflame with King Philip's War. To the men of early Massachusetts a war against the Indians was not simply a defensive move to prevent massacres from overwhelming their frontier towns and villages. It was an act of pious extermination, a crusade to be carried on relentlessly against a supernatural foe.

The first group of Puritan immigrants to New England had a curious superstition that persisted for nearly a century. They believed that the churches of Christ had succeeded in driving the Devil completely out of the old world. He and his forces would make a last stand in what they called "the frozen swamps of North America." They believed in a real, personified Devil who walked abroad in the world, could be seen and touched, and sometimes talked with. Usually described as "a black man," he could also display horns, hoofs, and a tail. Sometimes good Christians listened to him and were won to his side by promises of rich earthly rewards and supernatural power over their neighbors. Then they became witches, sworn to carry out his will. But the Indians were from birth the Devil's creatures. When they tried to kill off the white man, they were not only protecting their hunting grounds; they were carrying on the Devil's work in the world and fighting against Christ and the church. Hence, to slaughter the red Indians was a holy duty.

On both sides the war between the English settlers and King Philip's Wampanoags that troubled New England during Cotton Mather's youth proved both vicious and bloody. With Philip ignominiously killed, the Indians retreated a little farther, and the farms and villages spread deeper into the back country. A new Massachusetts began to grow up along the rivers that wound inland, among the western mountains. Rumors of it penetrated to Harvard Yard and the Old College, but did not arouse much interest there. Cotton Mather thought that he knew the dangers lurking in the red man, and though he diligently tried to convert him, he never changed his mind.

Nor did he change his mind about himself, though his college classmates refused to accept him at his own high value. Only twelve years old, innocent and credulous for all his learning, it came as a shock to him that he who beats his fellows in the classroom is often beaten by them in the yard outside. Already he had a confident belief in his own divine calling to the ministry. His family had always treated him with studious respect, and he believed that he was entitled to special respect because of his family.

But the rowdy young men at Cambridge took another view. They tormented him, sent him on humiliating errands and tried to trick him into blasphemy, cards, and dicing. Increase Mather had to ride hotly over from Boston and protest to President Oakes, which did not make Cotton any more popular. Sons of ministers mingled here with sons of captains, weavers, and wheelwrights, but they all expected to enter the ministry. It was to train ministers that the college had been founded some forty years before. Three of these young men brought grief to both Mathers in late life: John Leverett, who was chosen president of the college when Cotton himself wished desperately for this honor, and Thomas and William Brattle, whom he felt to be evil geniuses in every way.

After three years of such studies as arithmetic, geography, logic, politics, ethics, physics, Greek, Hebrew, Chaldee, and Syriac, the young scholar took his bachelor's degree and his master's degree soon afterward. For a time it seemed that he could never follow his father and grandfathers into the ministry because he had a speech impediment, probably due to nervousness, and stuttered badly. While trying to overcome his defect he studied medicine for a year or two, but by 1680 he was able to preach a sermon at his deceased grandfather's church in Dorchester. Ordained on May 13, 1685, as assistant to his father at the Second Church, he remained in its service all his life.

Always a family man at heart and very attractive to young women, with his slender figure, sensitive face, fashionable clothes, and neatly curled periwig, to say nothing of his reputation for piety, he set about choosing and courting a wife. In May, 1686, he married Abigail Phillips, a fifteen-year-old Charlestown girl of fitting attainments and orderly carriage, and took her to live in a house where Increase Mather dwelt for a time after his home burned in 1676. Returning as a bridegroom to the familiar rooms he had known in his boyhood, the young man walked devoutly through them, giving each one back to God and wishing it "made serviceable for his glory."

What was he like, this young man whom Abigail Phillips married, whose sermons set the pious all agog on Sunday, who walked familiarly through the streets of Boston, buttonholing every man he saw and exhorting him to behave piously? Well enough to look at him now, for Cotton Mather did not change as he grew older. Whatever he was, he became only more so: nervous, nearsighted, proud, sensitive, and intense, a firm believer in the glory of God and the special destiny of the Mather family. Frequently he prayed all night and fasted until ready to collapse from weakness. Sometimes in a rush of humility he would throw himself on "the dust of my study floor," which was probably a figure of speech and not a reflection on Mrs. Mather's excellent housekeeping. He enjoyed performing acts of kindness for the poor and depraved as well as for his more respectable neighbors. He held meetings nearly every night for various groups—men, women, young people, and married couples—to discuss scripture with them, pray, and advise them on how to achieve more godly living.

He loved the new generation and had a deep faith in them, insisting that he wanted to write something that should do young people good when he was dead and gone. But he could be suspicious, harsh, and vituperative and refer to anyone who opposed him as "a vile monster." A great scholar but ignorant of everything that lay outside his books and his little world of Boston, he never traveled further from home than Plymouth or Salem. Master of ancient languages, he also knew French, Spanish, and the Indian tongue. Constantly preaching and writing, he had published by the time of his death some four hundred and fifty titles—sermons, pamphlets, tracts, and his great work, the *Magnalia Christi Americana,* a religious history of New England.

Cotton Mather possessed a great faculty for reading deep meaning into little things, and was always seeing prophetic announcements in the small events of everyday life. A sense of sin influenced all his thoughts, together with a high degree of superstition. When his tooth ached he believed that this happened to him because he had committed some sin with his mouth—gluttony, perhaps, or evil speaking. Fond of pointing out that lightning struck church steeples and ministers' houses more often than other buildings, he took this for a display of the Devil's wrath against Christendom.

Given to long argumentative prayers himself, he posted a

sign on the wall of his extensive library which read, "Be Brief." His overweening ambition did not grow less with the years, and disappointment made him bitter rather than mellow. Tedious and lugubrious, he found "Man's life is a life of labor, and usually it is a labor in vain."

About the time Cotton Mather set himself up for a married man, changes began that almost overwhelmed his small world. For many years the English government ignored the colonies. But now the colonies were thriving and growing more important. The last Stuart kings, Charles and James II, began to take an interest in them, particularly as a source of revenue. Massachusetts lost its charter, its only legal basis for existence, and English governors came over, first Randolph and then Sir Edmund Andros. They were tyrannical and unpopular with the people, until finally replaced, under the government of William and Mary, by Sir William Phipps, a native New Englander. But the old way of life had disappeared, never to return. Anglican services were now held, first in the town house, and then in an Anglican church which had been built. Christmas began to be celebrated. The Congregational ministers lost their political power and never regained it. Massachusetts ceased to be the Bible commonwealth its founders had intended, and the gradual changes that were to make it a part of our modern democracy began.

The Mathers took this hard and fought against it, though not with violence, counseling peaceful resistance rather than revolution. Increase went to England to try to procure a new charter. Cotton stayed at home and preached against the sinful ways coming in as the old social discipline relaxed—card playing, tavern haunting, and riotous behavior after dark in the streets of Boston.

Children were born to him, and he became increasingly famous for his scholarship and his tireless activity in administering the affairs of the Second Church during his father's absence. In 1688 began the phase of his life which has brought him the most criticism and which is the hardest for twentieth-century minds to understand.

To our less superstitious generation, a witch is a gaunt female figure in black with a pointed hat, riding a broomstick across a Halloween card; or perhaps a costumed guest at a masquerade party. But to Cotton Mather and the men of his time, in both the old world and the new, a witch was a creature endowed by the Devil with evil powers and a menace to the community where she dwelt. The witch—or wizard, if a man—could carry on a singlehanded campaign against her neighbors and work malicious mischief or worse. She could cause horses to go lame, wheels to fall off carts, and milk to keep from turning to butter in the churn. She could afflict cattle with disease and cause all sorts of pains and illnesses in human beings. She could pronounce a curse on anyone who offended her. People tended to remember the occasions when her words came true and forget those when they failed to be effective. Throughout the sixteenth and seventeenth centuries hundreds of men and women were put to death because the courts that tried them for witchcraft pronounced them guilty.

There were a great many superstitions, too, regarding these followers of the Devil. If thrown into water, they would float. If stuck with pins, they felt no pain. They could not repeat the Lord's Prayer, and they writhed in torment if they heard scripture read. They could see and talk with their Black

Master. Sometimes they joined in groups called "covens" and met on lonely hillsides to dance and hold obscene rites.

Occasional witchcraft trials had occurred in New England before the great outbreak in Salem. Cotton Mather studied them with interest, and he firmly believed in witchcraft just as we believe in radioactivity or nuclear fission. It was a fact of nature. He had seen it demonstrated, or thought he had. A common trick of the New England witches, according to accounts by their contemporaries, was to torment children, causing them to suffer fits, cramps, and spasms, to fling themselves about and leap into the air trying to soar like geese, crying all the while, " 'Tis Goody Cloyse—Corey—Procter—who afflicts me!" "It is the Devil coming to me in the shape of Sarah Good!" Then the ministers and the court would hasten to seize and question these innocent women thus named and try to get them to confess to tormenting the children, to allowing the Devil to appear in their shapes, to committing the sin of witchcraft. If they confessed, they were usually released with a warning. If they refused to confess, they were searched for witchmarks, harried and roughly handled, perhaps hanged or left to languish and die in prison.

Cotton Mather and his fellow ministers who stood firmly behind the witchcraft trials did not so much fear bodily harm to the victims. They feared for the corrupting of immortal souls and for the expanding of the Devil's power. Therefore they rose like an army against the accused witches. Several children were afflicted in Boston, and Mather took two of them into his own home so that he could observe their fits, listen to their outcries, and question them, trying to learn more about the workings of the Devil's plot to take over New England.

To our modern eyes it seems that the children were hysterical, malicious, seeking attention, eager to take revenge on those who had offended them in some slight way. At Salem there is more than a hint that canny and purposeful adults may have stage-managed the business. When the ministers gathered in Mather's house to watch the children cry and thrash about, they questioned him closely as to a victim's daily routine. "Does she sleep?" "Hardly at all." "Does she eat?" "She does not eat and drinks nothing but rum." If this were the case, surely erratic behavior might be expected without benefit of witchcraft.

The terrible story of what happened in Salem between September and March, 1692, has been told many times, and need not be repeated here, save to mention the part that Cotton Mather played in it. And there is some disagreement as to what his part was. Everyone agrees that he displayed great excitement when he heard that a group of young girls had become terribly afflicted in Salem village. They named certain goodwives of the countryside as the witches who afflicted them. These women were promptly jailed, and a special court was set up to handle their cases. Mather visited Salem, witnessed some of the trials, and wrote a vivid book called *Wonders of the Invisible World,* which includes a whole study of the subject of witchcraft and makes plain his beliefs about it. Certainly he preached with zeal that great diligence should be employed to stamp out this evil. It is to his credit, however, that he did warn against accepting "spectral evidence." This meant that since it was not yet certain whether the Devil could assume the shape of an innocent person, evidence of the Devil's appearing in a person's shape should not be enough to convict him.

But at times Mather seems to have accepted spectral evidence himself, and he made a dramatic appearance at one execution. At the hanging of George Burroughs, a former minister, he rode up and harangued the crowd who had begun to murmur against the executions and wished to proceed more cautiously. After hearing Mather's eloquence they felt reassured, flung Burroughs's body into a rough crevice between the rocks, and went on to hang more innocent people. By the end of the summer Essex County jails were full of the accused. Nineteen witches had been hanged, and one wizard had been pressed to death by having stones heaped upon him.

Then suddenly the hysteria died away as swiftly as it had arisen. The special court held no more trials. One by one the prisoners were released and allowed to creep home. Some said that the afflicted children had cried out against people too highly placed in the colony, including the wife of Governor Phipps. Some said that the natural common sense of man and his humanity to his neighbors had returned with the cooling breezes of autumn. But others lamented that the work should cease, that the "firebrands of hell" should no longer swing from the gallows, and some evidence places Cotton Mather with this group. One authority has interpreted a letter of his to mean that he wanted to start a movement in Boston that would equal or surpass the Salem horror. He did not openly retract, as some others did, but in the later years of his life he lamented his action. If we feel inclined to judge him harshly, we should remember that we are really blaming him for being no wiser than the world he lived in—a charge that could be brought against many who condemn this Puritan.

One interesting historical theory suggests that the ministers of Massachusetts planned the witchcraft episode in an attempt to demonstrate how much the colony needed them and their prayers. This, they thought, would restore their lost political power. But if there was such a plot it is doubtful if Mather took part in it. He believed too sincerely.

Cotton Mather lived for more than thirty years after the Great Delusion at Salem village. In a sense they were declining years, for he suffered many more disappointments than successes. He and his father never won back the political power they had enjoyed under the old charter government. They tried very hard to do it and approached succeeding governors so officiously that they became unpopular with each administration. After 1706 they gave up the effort and devoted themselves to preaching, study, and pastoral duties. Increase lost the presidency of Harvard College because he refused to reside in Cambridge. Every time the post became vacant—almost up to the day of his death—Cotton hoped to be appointed to it and considered it a wickedness that he never was. They opposed the founding of the more liberal Brattle Street Church under the auspices of John Leverett and Thomas and William Brattle, all Cotton's old schoolfellows. Of this church Cotton wrote in January, 1700:

> I see Satan beginning a terrible Shake unto the Churches of New England, and the *Innovators* that have sett up a New Church in Boston, (a *New* one indeed!) have made a Day of Temptation among us. The men are Ignorant, Arrogant, Obstinate and full of malice and slander, and they fill the Land with Lyes, in the misrepresentations whereof I am a very singular sufferer. Wherefore I set apart this day again for prayer in my study to cry mightily unto God.

It was in fact his custom to spend every Saturday in his study communing with the Lord of Heaven and Earth and

His Radiant Angels. Cotton Mather spoke directly to God, and he believed that God answered him. Perhaps no other man has ever walked more closely hand in hand with his deity.

But all this closeness did not keep his enemies from thriving and their church along with them, and Mather came reluctantly to terms with it. About this time, too, he received perhaps the cruelest wound his public life had to bear. Robert Calef, a merchant of Boston, who with the Brattles had opposed the witchcraft trials, now brought out a book called *More Wonders of the Invisible World,* attacking Cotton Mather sharply for his attitude toward the suspected witches and their victims. Calef, a very enlightened man for his time, took a skeptical view of all witchcraft, and he found Mather's conduct not only ridiculous but evil. The book caused a great uproar in Boston. Calef's supporters jeered triumphantly, and the Mathers hissed back. A rumor exists that copies of the book were burned in Harvard Yard. To read the two books, Cotton's *Wonders* and Calef's *More Wonders,* is to go on a real adventure into seventeenth-century America, as well as into the minds of the two authors. They can be recommended to anyone interested in the study of thought or the history of superstition.

But God was not through with chastening his faithful servant. In the late fall of 1702 Cotton Mather wrote, "At last the black day arrives." He then describes the deathbed of his wife, Mrs. Abigail Mather.

So Two Hours before my Lovely Consort Expired, I kneeled by her Bed-Side and I took into my two Hands, a dear Hand, the dearest in the World. With her thus in my Hands, I solemnly and sincerely gave her up unto the Lord: and in token of my Real RESIGNATION, I gently putt her out of my

Hands, and Laid away a most Lovely Hand, Resolving that I would never touch it any more. This was the Hardest, and perhaps the bravest Action, that ever I did.

No one remained long widowed in those days when both a man and a woman were so urgently needed to perform the daily tasks of every household. Abigail had been hardly two months dead before a fashionable young woman of Boston came to see the bereaved minister. She told him frankly that she admired him for his person and his piety and would like to be joined to both of them. Cotton found himself strongly drawn to her. They visited each other, exchanged gifts, and talked of their future together. But when Increase heard about it he objected violently. Gossip seethed in the congregation of the Second Church. The girl was reported to be gay, frivolous, and of light behavior, if not actually sinful—certainly no fit wife for a reverend minister. She and her mother protested, and poor Cotton agonized.

Some writers have felt her to be the woman whom he most truly loved, a creature of wit and intelligence who could understand his deeper side and be more than a simple housewife, mother of children. She moves vividly through the pages of his diary. We can almost smell her dainty perfume and hear the rustle of her silken skirts as she wooed her scholarly minister with all the ardor of Priscilla seeking John Alden. But unlike Priscilla she did not succeed. Cotton Mather took for his second wife Elizabeth Hubbard, a respectable widow.

He seems to have been well enough pleased with Elizabeth, but she died in 1713. His third wife, widow Lydia George, proved to be a termagant, and a real crown of thorns, though perhaps not actually mad, as Cotton swore she was. Jealous of his writings, she would hide and burn them. The pair quarreled constantly, and in trying to settle her daughter's stormy financial affairs, the poor minister found himself involved in debt and a lawsuit.

If his domestic life after 1713 brought him little happiness, he did achieve honors abroad which added to his local reputation. The University of Glasgow made him a doctor of divinity, and the Royal Society elected him to membership because of his writings and observations on natural history—in which Newbury's double-headed snake was no doubt fully described.

In 1721 a great smallpox epidemic broke out in Boston. Cotton immediately moved to protect the inhabitants of his city. He had read in a paper of the Royal Society a description of inoculation, the forerunner of our modern vaccination, and he urged that it be tried at once. All the Boston doctors vehemently opposed it except Dr. Zabdiel Boylston who inoculated his own children and then Mather's young son, Samuel. Foes of Mather and modern medical science raised "a horrid clamor." Some unknown hand actually threw a sort of bomb into the minister's house at midnight—an iron ball with a fuse and powder attached which failed to explode. To it was tied a note which read, "COTTON MATHER, You Dog, Dam you: I'll inoculate you with this and a Pox to you." Mather describes the incident with such gusto that one feels he enjoyed being a martyr.

His later years were full of unhappiness caused by his children. Though he fathered fifteen, only two survived him. Increase, his first son to attain manhood, turned out to be no pride and joy. No scholar, unfit for Harvard or the ministry, unable to settle to any business, he became involved in difficulties and scandal and finally drowned in the West Indies. Katy, the favorite daughter, died in 1716. He had loved his children deeply and reared them with a gentleness uncommon in early New England; he had done his best to educate them. Thriftless "Creasy" studied music and fencing along with his Latin. Katy not only was skilled in needlework and housewifery, but knew music, sacred geography, and Hebrew.

Preaching and writing almost to the very end, Cotton Mather died the day after his sixty-fifth birthday, February 13, 1728. "My last enemy has come," he wrote to his physician, "I would say, my best friend." "Now I have nothing more to do here," he said a few hours before his death. "My will is entirely swallowed up in the will of the Lord."

If we cannot understand him, cannot always like him, we can remember him for his good qualities: his intensity and his devotion to God, his kindliness, and his concern for the young. We remember his scholarship and intellectual curiosity, his own fine memory, and the zeal with which he toiled all his days to save the souls of men. Born within a decade after the death of Plymouth's Governor Bradford, and dying only a few months before the birth of the Revolutionary general John Stark, his life is a link between those who settled America and those who made it a modern nation. His life is so much the life of a man of his time that it provides a good introduction to a study of the America he lived in.

When Benjamin Franklin was an old man he wrote in a letter to Cotton Mather's son, Dr. Samuel Mather:

When I was a boy, I met with a book, entitled *Essays to do Good,* which I think was written by your father. It had been so little regarded by a former possessor, that several leaves of it were torn out; but the remainder gave me such a turn of thinking, as to have influenced my conduct through life; for I have always set a greater value on the character of a *doer of good,* than on any other kind of reputation; and if I have been, as you seem to think, a useful citizen, the public owes the advantage of it to that book. . . . It is more than sixty years since I left Boston, but I remember well both your father and grandfather, having heard them both in the pulpit, and seen them in their houses. The last time I saw your father was in the beginning of 1724, when I visited him after my first trip to Pennsylvania. He received me in his library, and on my taking leave showed me a shorter way out of the house through a narrow passage, which was crossed by a beam overhead. We were still talking as I withdrew, he accompanying me behind, and I turning partly towards him, when he said hastily, *"Stoop, stoop!"* I did not understand him, till I felt my head hit against the beam. He was a man that never missed any occasion of giving instruction, and upon this he said to me, *"You are young and have the world before you. STOOP as you go through it, and you will miss many hard thumps!"*

This advice, thus beat into my head, has frequently been of use to me; and I often think of it when I see pride mortified, and misfortunes brought upon people by their carrying their heads too high.

And so it was that Cotton Mather had his wish, to write something that should do young people good when he was dead and gone.

Chapter 4

———⟨∘⟩———

JONATHAN EDWARDS

The circling woods were bright with flame and scarlet on that autumn day, October 3, 1703, and the farmers in the little Connecticut River town of East Windsor had stripped their fields and brought the harvest home. Reverend Timothy Edwards turned away from his wife's bedside. Happiness shone in his grave eyes as he watched the river flowing blackly westward. Down that river lay Hartford, and word must go to his father, a prosperous merchant there; upriver, too, to Esther's father, Reverend Solomon Stoddard at Northampton, Massachusetts. She had finally borne a son after giving him four daughters—and he did not know of the six daughters who would follow. He would name this child Jonathan, he thought—not a family name, but a Biblical one, with a worth and dignity of its own.

They were a pious couple, these two, who welcomed the newcomer to the low parsonage with its overhanging second story and great square hearth; not only pious, but possessed of good common sense and spirited personalities, well able to provide the sort of home background where a lad of genius could thrive. Timothy was a Harvard graduate, and Esther, learned beyond most women of her time, ably managed the household and directed the children's studies when her husband had to be away from home.

Jonathan grew up a sturdy youngster, tall, with a broad forehead, finely cut features, and low, impressive voice. Woods stretched out on three sides of the country town that was his world during his first thirteen years of life: woods, and fields to be tilled, river meadows where his father taught him how to cut hay. A small-town minister never earned enough salary to pay for all the shoes, sugar, bacon, and firewood, the many needs of his family; never enough to add to his meager collection of well-loved and necessary books. So he had usually to maintain a farm as well and care for at least one horse, pigs, chickens, and cattle. Reverend Timothy ran his farm profitably, but without enthusiasm. He forgot important details sometimes, because his mind preferred to busy itself with scholarship, sermons, and parish activities.

That his only son should help him in his pursuits was taken for granted, and Jonathan accepted his father's way of life, never desiring to change it for any other. Sitting in the parlor with the children of the village while his parents heard their lessons, he began to look forward to the day when he, too, would be a minister of God.

His books meant a great deal to him, but so, too, did the world of nature beyond the leaded windowpanes. The moon and the stars in the sky; rainbows after a storm; the grasses in the fields and the ferns in the forest; most of all the living creatures whose habits he loved to observe—all these attracted him, not only for themselves, but for the meaning which lay concealed in them. He made his observations with the careful and judicious eye of a scientist, but the end of his study was not science. Beyond the leaf and the flower, he worshipped the idea of the leaf and the flower which he felt existed in the mind of God. From childhood he was a mystic, a religious spirit, and a philosopher.

Most of the houses stood along "the Street," and just across a small ravine from his father's meetinghouse loomed the stockade built in the old days as a refuge against Indian attacks. Behind the parsonage the land sloped down to a brook with the forest beyond it, and across the river the steeple of Windsor Church rose through the treetops. A canoe trip to hear a sermon at Windsor was an adventure full of danger and excitement. And after danger and excitement came the need for solitude and prayer. Jonathan built a small shelter of boughs in the depths of the marshy woodland where he could retire to pray and seek God. Later he allowed other boys to share its privacy for the same purpose, going even deeper into the woods when he needed to be quite alone. In the fall of 1716 when he rode off to enter Yale College he was by no means a young recluse, but he sometimes wrote home that he had to force himself to close his books in the evening and seek the company of his fellows.

Today the gray stone towers of Yale College at New Haven have an everlasting look, as if they have always been there, but not one of them existed in Jonathan Edwards's freshman year. Nor was it definitely decided that New Haven would be the seat of the new college established about the time of Jonathan's birth because some of the Connecticut clergy considered Harvard too newfangled and liberal. Books had been given, but they were held in storage at Saybrook while Hartford, New Haven, and Wethersfield also competed for the honor. Classes met in at least three of the rival towns. The

Assembly had voted five hundred pounds for a building to hold both books and students, but where was it to be built?

Jonathan enrolled at New Haven, but after a few weeks his entire class moved to Wethersfield and placed itself under the tutelage of Elisha Williams, a brilliant young Harvard graduate and a relative of the Edwards family. Life here was not so different from what it had been in East Windsor. With no dormitories available, the students boarded round about in the homes of the townspeople. Hard study, early bedtime, and intense Sabbath keeping were nothing new to most of the lads, certainly not to Jonathan. Unfortunately they could not remain aloof from their elders' dispute about the seat of the college. Representatives of the interested towns kept intruding on their classes, urging them to transfer to one place or the other. Eventually New Haven triumphed and the books from Saybrook were transferred by oxcart to the new "College House" facing the green. Nor did they have a safe journey. Enraged Saybrook men overset the carts, and many valuable books and manuscripts were "conveyed away by unknown hands and never could be found again." We can imagine what the sedate and scholarly young Edwards must have thought of such goings-on!

During his senior year he lived at New Haven and enjoyed the post of college butler, a position of honor. Standing at one end of the dining hall, it was his task to fill the mugs and dole out equal portions of bread and beef. He had a quarrel with a young cousin, Elisha Mix, and wrote home to his father. Reverend Timothy immediately wrote to Elisha's family upbraiding them. Through all their lives the Edwardses, both father and son, had a strict sense of justice and pastoral authority, a lack of humor, and a compelling desire to correct the behavior of others by the standards of their own superior self-righteousness. This often caused them to walk a hard and thorny way.

Jonathan remained at Yale for six years of intensive study, and during this time he found his own world, which was to be always a world of ideas rather than of men. Not for him were the pranks of the other lads—stealing pigs, breaking windows, night walking, card playing, cursing, and swearing. Locke's *Essay On Human Understanding* brought him the inspiration and the method he most needed for engaging his mind in the pure process of abstract thought. It led him to the perception of a natural law governing all things, into a realm of universal order and beauty where not all of us are able to follow him.

Perhaps more important was what he considered his conversion. This happened when he was seventeen and covered a period of many anguished months when he felt sometimes as if God were shaking him over the pit of hell. He began to see his earlier devotions, the hut in the swamp, the lonely walks in the woods of East Windsor, as merely an outward showing of piety, the dead husk containing no rich fruit of true religious experience within. During these months of struggle he discovered within himself a "new sense of things," a knowledge of the divine glory existing everywhere. He felt his soul to be diffused with a sense of the Divine Being, "a Calm, sweet Abstraction of Soul from all the Concerns of this World." His new knowledge kindled a sweet burning in his heart, an ardor of soul that he knew not how to express. He saw the glory of God in the moon and heard His voice in the thunder.

Now he was truly God's and could bring God's word to the

people. Let the lads who pushed and shouted on New Haven green call him a stiff-necked prude and spoilsport. He was the citizen of another kingdom. He had entered through God's mercy on another way of life.

In 1722 he left the college, once again in a state of turmoil because its leaders had turned Episcopalian, and went to minister to a small Presbyterian congregation in New York City. It met in a building on William Street. Not far off lay the wharves where ships from England, France, Holland, and the West Indies put in, bringing strange cargoes, strange men, and new ideas. Jonathan could have lingered in the cobbled squares to watch a sailor swagger by with a cockatoo on his shoulder, or a fine-coated merchant cross himself with a gesture from an older religion than his own. Here the farm boy from Connecticut had a chance for the first time to become part of a larger world. But instead he confined himself to the little group on William Street and read the Bible aloud with his landlord, John Smith, a simple currier from the docks.

That he loved his first little flock we know, because his letters expressed so much sadness on leaving them, but they were too poor to support a minister. In April, 1723, he returned to his father's house, expecting to be called to the Bolton church that autumn. And so he was. Salary, firewood, pastureland, and a homestead were provided for him, but a better appointment offered itself. He made his choice, not out of ambition, but through a sense that in doing as he did he followed God's will. On May 21, 1724, he was appointed senior tutor at Yale College.

This meant the incurring of a great burden of activities and responsibility. Edwards had to arrange and supervise many administrative details besides his teaching. Discipline, always a problem where lively young men are concerned, took up much of his time. When the new tutor wished to meditate on God, he had, instead, to rebuke his charges for intemperance, hallooing, firing off guns, and ringing the college bell unseasonably. He discharged his duties faithfully, aided by his own excellent habits and sense of order, but found that he now had "abundant Reason to be convinced of the Troublesomeness and Vexations of this World, and that it would never be any other Kind of World."

In September, 1725, he suffered a severe illness and nearly lost his life. After that the abounding health of his boyhood never returned. He became subject to frequent attacks of fever and had to confine himself to a sparse and simple diet. He went back to Yale for a brief time, but his next adventure already awaited him. In a sense it had awaited him ever since he was born. He had inherited it.

Up in the little Massachusetts town of Northampton a distinguished career was drawing to its close. Every Sunday when the people poured out of their weather-beaten, unpainted houses and climbed Meeting House Hill to listen to the Reverend Solomon Stoddard, as the older ones had been doing for some fifty-five years, they realized afresh that he would soon need a successor.

And where could they find such another? What worthy young man trained in the rich, cultured cities of the coast would accept a pulpit in this backwoods village of fertile river meadows and rough sheep pastures with the mountains looking down? No highroad led in or out, only the river; and the forest menaced on all sides. Yet here lived Christian souls, and they were used to the spiritual guidance of a master. Solomon Stoddard had been a great man, holding his own like a black rock through half a century of Massachusetts religious controversy. Where would they find another such—and yet, was there not a young man of the blood? Did not Reverend Solomon have a grandson, pious, according to all reports, a tutor at the new college in Connecticut Colony?

And so Jonathan Edwards was ordained in the church at Northampton in February, 1727. Thus the boundaries of his life were set. Back country Massachusetts was to be the scene of his successes and failures—only at the very end would he struggle beyond it.

At the start of his career not only young Jonathan but all his fellow ministers would have shaken their heads over the condition of the New England churches and pronounced religion to be in a sad decline. The church was no longer the political power that it had been in the early days of New England. Religion did not play such an important part in the daily lives of the people. Men still attended Sunday service and Thursday lecture, but they did not have a sense of walking every day with God as their grandfathers had had. Instead of sitting at home to study the Bible and pray for a state of grace, the young people went dashing off to husking bees, sleighing parties, and singing school. Everyone was busy opening up the new lands to the west and enjoying more comfortable ways of life.

New immigrants had come among them who did not have the religious devotion and intensity of the old comers. And in some few ways the churches had grudgingly adapted to the changing times. Most of the clergy resisted this bitterly. They complained that there was "a dying spirit in New England to the ways of God," "a decay upon the very vitals of religion."

They constantly lamented the old days and the old piety, seemingly gone forever.

These congregations were not like the early congregations when New England had "come alive with such a body of pious people as was never before seen upon this earth." God was not pleased with this new sinful generation, they said, and showed his displeasure by causing various disasters—an epidemic of the throat-ail, a blast destroying the wheat, or a boat burned in Boston Harbor. And their lamenting and upbraiding only served to estrange men further. What New England needed was a great awakening of religious fervor, a new sense of the almighty power of God. But how was this to be brought about?

In the early days only those who had received divine revelation were considered as having entered into the Covenant and thus become worthy of enjoying the full privileges of the church. Around 1662 the "Halfway Covenant" came into favor, and Solomon Stoddard supported it. This was a modification of early severity and allowed decent and orderly members of the community to be received into the church, even though they had experienced no revelation. Also their children could be baptized. The only sacrament denied them was that of the Lord's Supper.

Later Mr. Stoddard carried the practice further and admitted everyone to the sacrament table, arguing that it might do them good and lead them to holiness and personal experience of God. Many clergymen protested, but he stood his ground and the practice spread. Jonathan Edwards had read his grandfather's books and in the beginning took no exception to the theory. For two years the two men served the church together, sitting side by side on Sunday morning, though the more tedious parish work, visiting the sick and catechizing the children, fell to Jonathan. Then on February 11, 1729, his grandfather died, and he stood forth alone.

Yet not quite alone, for he had taken unto himself a most amiable wife only five months after his ordination. She was Sarah Pierrepont, of New Haven, whom he had met while a student at Yale, daughter of a prominent minister and descendant of Reverend Thomas Hooker, who helped to found the colony. Beautiful she was, possessed of deep spiritual gifts, but also practical, able to manage a household and move easily in society as Jonathan never could. "She is beloved of the Great Being who made and rules the World," her husband wrote of her, and she could experience religious ecstasy as deeply as he.

The young couple bought a house on quiet King Street, amply provided with salary, ten acres of pastureland, and forty acres up the river. When he fell ill the people built him "a good large barn." They seemed to have a deep love and respect for their young pastor and to "take great comfort in his ministry."

As the years went by and children were born to them, little notices among his papers list household purchases and memoranda that tell us much about their way of life: "clergyman's buttons," "three pounds for a hat," "eleven pounds for a gold locket and chain." The Edwards family did not believe in luxury and display, but they believed in being well dressed and well fed. Bills for spelling books, cables of thread, thimbles, three yards of lutestring, a silk handkerchief, a silk ribbon for Sarah, a broom, a mousetrap, "one child's plaything," groceries and chocolate; a bill from Dr. Mather for two bloodlettings; a reminder to bring home Lucy's shoes.

Both his father and his grandfather had preached their sermons without notes, as Jonathan himself was to do later, but
during his first decade at Northampton he read them aloud,
keeping one finger on the page as he went along. We still have
some five hundred tiny stitched booklets wherein his sermons
are written in fine script. His style of preaching was quiet and
forceful rather than bombastic, but it held every man's attention. He could paint arresting word pictures, but always in
Biblical terms rather than in the familiar speech and scenes
of Northampton. He himself said that his style was plain and
unfashionable, and he certainly did not try to beautify it so
far that the meaning could be lost in poetic expression. The
lyrical sermons of his youth became more prosaic as he grew
older, devoted to ethics and piety rather than divine inspiration.

So he went on, much as other country ministers of deep
faith and scholarly learning, known beyond his own parish
only for one rather famous sermon he preached in Boston in
1731. This was his first work to appear in print and commanded much attention. As a whole, the Massachusetts clergy
applauded it. This young man, they saw, had followed divine
guidance which led sometimes into strange ways, but not so
with Jonathan Edwards. Contemplation, study, and maturity
had brought him back to the earlier, stricter ways of Calvin-
ism. In his eyes the sinner could not save himself by an impressive list of good works. If the grace of God shone not
within him, he was doomed. Salvation could not be earned, it
could be conferred only from on high.

Late in the fall of 1733 the young people of Northampton
began to show a willingness to give ear to their minister, and
an unusual spirit of piety appeared among them. Eagerly

Jonathan Edwards sought to encourage it. When he preached a sermon against mirth-making and company-keeping on Sunday evenings, they immediately gave up those pleasures. Encouraged by this, he kept on to exhort his people to hope for divine grace within, to cease trying to achieve salvation by good works. Good works were to be performed, surely, but they counted for nothing without the inner illumination of the spirit.

Not everyone agreed with him, and rifts and quarrels appeared in the parish. Edwards responded by preaching harshly, including a roll call of the sins of the town that he said would surely kindle divine wrath and shut its people out from God's mercy, condemn them to eternal torment.

Indignation and then terror woke in the hearts of his neighbors. Was this the kindly minister they had always known? They had always believed him, and must they not believe him now? "What shall I do to be saved?" men were asking each other in the street after service. On Monday morning they thronged, quaking, about the parsonage door, demanding, "What shall I do to be saved?"

All the town was suddenly astir about religion; all ordinary business was put aside. Was this the great revival the clergy had been hoping for? Jonathan Edwards exulted that it might be so, and he the one to lead it. He toiled night and day, holding private conferences, meeting with small groups, leading prayers and hymn singing. In November came the first conversion. One sinful young woman swore that she felt the divine light rising in her heart and embraced the faith. Then another joined her, and another. On a single Sunday an even hundred were taken into the fold, including little children, some of them hysterical with terror, fearful of the flaming hell they had heard their minister describe.

And not only the children suffered from hysteria. In the spring of 1735 Northampton folk had endured so much nervous tension, so much fear and ecstasy, that they could stand no more, and a wave of suicides broke out. This sobered the community and brought them back to the more prosaic levels of everyday life. Jonathan Edwards sighed regretfully and set about plans for a new meetinghouse that should be large enough to house the three hundred converts the awakening had brought. He was as yet unaware that the town would never love him quite as it had before.

About this time he began to make powerful enemies outside of Northampton. The Massachusetts Assembly censured the Hampshire Association for jailing Robert Breck, a young liberal chosen by the Springfield church to be its pastor. Jonathan Edwards prepared the defense of the Association, and Breck's friends held this against him for the rest of his life.

Then came the eventful year, 1740, which changed the whole aspect of religion in America. In Edwards's church as in many more, there had been moments of excitement during the past decade, stirrings and faint signs that men felt the need of God and were ready to turn to him with all the ardor and urgency their grandfathers had shown in the old days. But it took a stranger from beyond the seas to bring this about, a man of powerful dramatic gifts, if lacking in intellect and true spirituality.

George Whitefield arrived in Boston that September, heralded by advance reports of his astonishing success in England as a popular preacher. Staid Massachusetts had never seen his like. Here a sermon was a scholarly exercise, a statement of doctrine, followed by proof and application, delivered forcefully perhaps, but with restraint and dignity. Whitefield had no dignity. "He would even go so far as to rave, stare, foam, and beat his breast." He wept and laughed and sang in the pulpit. He could stir up men's emotions and play upon them as upon the taut strings of a violin. And Massachusetts men loved it. They waited in the rain to hear him. They waited in early morning darkness. They jammed the meetinghouses and poured in from every tiny village to overflow Boston Common. He struck them with awe, and he struck them with terror, and one by one they came rushing forward repenting, weeping, shrieking, pleading to be saved. George Whitefield in that New England autumn brought about the religious revival that has come to be known as the "Great Awakening." He established the dubious technique of mass hysteria that remains even today the mainstay of the revivalist.

Whitefield spent four days at the parsonage in Northampton and preached to Jonathan Edwards's congregation. Then he was gone in a trail of fiery eloquence across Connecticut, and the countryside could settle back to religious lethargy once more. But no! The native clergy had seen the way. Sermons were hastily constructed and stowed away in saddlebags. The ministry took to the highroads and bridle paths. Visiting one another's congregations with the novelty of the outsider to aid them, they carried on what Whitefield had begun, with Edwards himself well to the fore.

Perhaps his most famous sermon was preached at Enfield in July, 1741. He described for his listeners the terrible wrath of God, falling suddenly and unsuspected upon wicked men. And his words and gestures and the tone of his voice made each man feel himself to be a sinner, feel that at any moment the wrath would fall and sweep him away in eternal flame. One witness of the scene reported that there was "a great moaning and crying out through ye whole house. What shall I do to be saved? Oh I am going to Hell! Oh what shall I do for Christ, etc., etc. Ye minister was obliged to desist—ye cries and shrieks were piercing and amazing."

But as with so much in nature the strength of the Great Awakening—its emotional intensity—was its weakness. Its very success brought about its death. The hysteria swelled to a point where the clergy could no longer pretend it to be anything but unhealthy and ridiculous. They suddenly discovered that while they were gadding about filling other pulpits, their own flocks were getting out of hand. Whitefield had encouraged people to rise in the audience and testify to their own religious experience as the spirit moved them. This privilege was now carried to the point of vicious abuse. Bands of unlettered and violent young men roamed from town to town, bursting in uninvited wherever service was in progress, uttering cries of rude vigor rather than piety. In Ipswich Church one man shouted "Come to Christ," for a steady half hour, while "a mean fellow preached," and an old woman in a rear pew denounced lawyers. Chaos seemed loosened upon the churches of New England.

To make things worse, in 1744 Whitefield again visited America. Many ministers now turned against him, and he was forbidden such pulpits as those of Harvard and Yale. Thus attacked, he defended himself. Controversy broke out, and the clergy lined up on one side or the other. Those who favored his aims and methods were called "New Lights," while the "Old Lights" sought to return to more decorous ways.

The Mayflower in Plymouth Harbor, painted by Gribble, an English artist

Statue of William Bradford

John Winthrop

Statue of Roger Williams in Providence, Rhode Island

Portrait of Cotton Mather

Picture of Jonathan Edwards taken from an old print

Below: Portrait of Paul Revere by J. S. Copley

Courtesy, Museum of Fine Arts, Boston

Portrait of John Hancock by
J. S. Copley

John Adams, about 1797,
from a crayon portrait by
Saint-Mémin

Portrait of Ethan Allen
by Donald A. Baker

Portrait of Gen. John
Stark, by Samuel F. B.
Morse, 1816

Courtesy of Macbeth Galleries, New York

Capt. Samuel Morey

The home Morey designed for his family

Eli Whitney

Jonathan Edwards was considered by everyone except himself to be a New Light, but he insisted that he followed a middle course. He regretted the excesses and abuses, but he felt that they should be ignored in view of the many conversions, the new importance religion had come to play in so many lives. He believed that this was only the beginning, and that the good work would go on. He explained his position in two treatises, *The Distinguishing Marks of a Work of the Spirit of God* and *Some Thoughts Concerning the Present Revival of Religion in New England*. And he became engaged in a pamphlet controversy with Thomas Clapp, rector of Yale College. Clapp believed that Edwards had entered into a conspiracy with Whitefield to place English ministers in American pulpits. Whitefield had mentioned the matter to Edwards, but that was as far as it went. But the interchange with Clapp caused much bitterness. After that Edwards no longer attended Yale commencements. Instead he went to Princeton.

Troubles were besetting him in his own parish. For some years he had experienced difficulty in collecting his salary. The village gossips whispered that the parsonage family lived too high. How could they afford to entertain so many visitors, to set such a good table, to order beaver hats and feminine trinkets from Boston—and to buy all those books? In vain Edwards argued that he sought no display or luxury, only the dignity suitable to a minister of God. They granted him money, but the complaints went on.

Then in 1744 came the unfortunate incident of the "bad book." Five or six of the older boys got hold of a manual of instruction for midwives supposed to contain medical knowledge harmful to young minds. The book was kept in secret hiding places and passed from hand to hand among both boys and girls. Edwards laid the matter before the church and appointed a committee to investigate and pass censure. Then he made the mistake of reading a list of the names of the young folk who must appear before the committee. Included were innocent witnesses as well as those supposedly guilty, with no distinction between them. All Northampton went into an uproar. Children of the most prominent and godly families were branded with public shame. The small scandal made a mighty noise, and Jonathan Edwards won the undying hatred of his former friends because he had attacked their young.

For three months the hearings went on, ending with the confession of the ringleaders and the estrangement of the younger generation from the church. While they were waiting to be examined, instead of hanging repentant heads, they climbed trees to peer at the girls locked in upper chambers, played leapfrog on the minister's lawn, and lounged across to the tavern to order mugs of flip.

But the case grew to have more than local importance. It raised the question of just how far parish authority over private behavior could really extend. Discussion spread from town to town, from pulpit to pulpit, and was not settled in Jonathan Edwards's time. His own behavior in the matter earned him his reputation as a stern, unrelenting disciplinarian, and he certainly deserved it. But his notes reveal a surprising uncertainty in his heart. Would he have done better, he asked himself, if he had talked with the children privately?

For the next four years gossip and money troubles followed him. No new converts joined the church. He felt that he had come on a dull, declining time. But the lamps in his study burned late as he prepared his important work, *Treatise*

Concerning Religious Affections. In this he examined the true nature of religious experience and tried to make plain that religion was a matter of the heart rather than the mind, a deep experience of God. Turning alike from the antics of men like Whitefield and the cold scholarly logic of the Old Lights, he sought a middle course, more appealing to those of our own day. And he wrote beautifully of the revelation of God to his creatures, which is such that the natural, unconverted man can discern

> . . . nothing of it any more than a man without the sense of tasting can conceive of the sweet taste of honey; or a man without the sense of hearing can conceive of the melody of a tune; or a man born blind can have a notion of the beauty of the rainbow. . . . All who are truly religious are not of this world.

But the life of the study was not all. Swiftly now he grew apart from his people. When he tried to "purify the Lord's table" and refuse the sacrament to those who had not experienced divine revelation, the community turned against him. He could not set the clock back. He could not take away the religious privileges Northampton had enjoyed for almost a century. The church members voted to dismiss him from their pulpit. A church council met to confirm their act, and his old opponent Robert Breck served on it, voting, of course, against him. On July 2, 1750, Edwards preached a moving farewell sermon.

Since his old flock could not find a replacement immediately he lingered in town, preaching now and then as they requested it. But quarrels still split the parish. His enemies feared he might try to organize a rival church. His friends could see no ready way to help him. All were relieved when he accepted a call to the Indian mission at Stockbridge and removed his family there in the fall of 1751.

Though bitterly hurt by his dismissal from the pulpit where he had labored for over a quarter of a century, Jonathan Edwards faced his new duties with courage and hopefulness. Alas, from the beginning the situation proved to be an impossible one. If Northampton had seemed remote and uncivilized after the life of New Haven, Stockbridge was far worse, a mere clearing in the forest with huts and wigwams clustered about the mission building that served two hundred and fifty Indian families and a few whites. All kinds of supplies were lacking, the founders of the mission numbered several of Edwards's old enemies, and they were more interested in establishing a profitable trading post than in saving souls. Struggle as conscientiously as he would, the man who had mastered Greek, Latin, and Hebrew could acquire only enough of the Indian tongue to conduct daily business. He could never preach in it, and thus left his hearers unmoved and bewildered.

Like most missionaries of his day, he looked on the Indians as souls to be saved, not living, breathing men like himself whose physical needs must be considered, their social customs respected. Edwards tried valiantly to run the mission well, but too heavy odds were against him. Then in 1754 war broke out. His flock drifted back into the forests to take up the tomahawk. A stockade had to be built around the parsonage, and refugees straggled in to tax Sarah Edwards's unfailing hospitality.

But neither the difficulties of everyday life in Stockbridge nor the continued attacks of his enemies could overwhelm the stubborn spirit within the frail body of the aging minister. Again as at Northampton, his quill pen and sheets of foolscap were at once his refuge and delight. First he issued a defense of his own conduct and a sharp answer to those who censured and disagreed with him. Then he went on to write his famous *Freedom of the Will* and other treatises.

Ever since coming over from England, the ministers of the new country had engaged in a mighty argument. Did man possess complete freedom of the will to do as he chose, or was he a creature entirely controlled by the will of God? Edwards now set down his thinking on this point in its final form that would represent him for all time. He believed that men did have control over their actions and could make choices, but that these choices were directed by motives outside man's control; that therefore the human will was passive. And he wrote reaffirming the doctrine of Original Sin—that the human race fell with Adam's fall and was guilty with his guilt.

Yet his religion was not all composed of vengeance and terror. It had comfort and beauty in it for the man who would open his heart to the workings of God. Finally, in *God's Last End in Creation,* he speculates on why God made the world, and emerges with the theory that it was made to partake of and reflect the divine glory, an everlasting process of exchange between God's creatures and Himself.

But the last chapter of Jonathan Edwards's life was not to be written in Stockbridge. In the fall of 1757 he received word of the death of his son-in-law, Aaron Burr, president of Princeton College. Almost at the same time he was offered the newly vacant position. It was an honor come almost too late. At first he refused it, pleading ill health, inadequacy, and the literary works he hoped to finish, but the trustees brushed aside his protests.

Across the frozen New England countryside and the great rivers about New York he journeyed to Princeton, arriving on February 16. He was inducted into office the same day and later preached a sermon, gave out questions in divinity to the senior class, and enjoyed a warm welcome on all sides. Since Princeton had suffered an outbreak of smallpox that winter, the new president underwent inoculation; he died of its effects on March 22, 1758.

In his last hours he resigned himself as always to the will of God, bade farewell to the two daughters who had nursed him, and left directions for his simple funeral. And to this day he lies in the quiet Princeton graveyard with its other presidents, in a stone coffin set atop the ground in the old way.

He was essentially of the old way, and still a New Light at the same time. He struggled desperately to perpetuate the grim, rigorous doctrines of Calvin, but in doing so he was able to infuse them with a new mysticism, a sense of beauty, eternal glory, and divine love. In spite of his self-righteousness, his narrow outlook and pitiless logic, to know the man is to feel that he truly walked with God. Strait is the gate and few they be that find it, but Jonathan Edwards was surely one.

He led the first religious revival in America and made emotional religion respectable. And the Great Awakening had an effect on American society beyond the province of religion. It opened men's mouths and taught them to "speak out in meeting," to speak for themselves, where every man's word was as good as every other man's. Without this earlier experience in democracy we might not have had the fearless, outspoken patriots of the Revolution.

And these men were coming on the scene now, men who worried about the state of their country rather than the state of their souls. As religion lost much of its power to restrict them, they turned their thoughts to the things of this world, but they did not lose idealism, or honor, or essential human goodness in doing so. They were new men shaped to a new time. Jonathan Edwards could never have played the dramatic, swift-paced part that history allotted to Paul Revere. But neither man is any the worse because of that. In the decade after Edwards's death the wheel swung; the ministers moved downward from the peak of importance, and the patriots swung upward, to be followed by the politicians, the inventors, and the business men.

Chapter 5

———◦∞◦———

PAUL REVERE

The name "Paul Revere" meant nothing to the thirteen-year-old Huguenot boy who stepped ashore on Boston's Long Wharf one sharp winter day in 1717. If he had heard it spoken he would scarcely have turned his head, though he might have thought it sounded somewhat like his own. Apollos Rivoire had left the vineyard country round Bordeaux, home of his family for generations. He came to America much as the Plymouth Pilgrims had come nearly a hundred years before. He wanted to escape from religious persecution and to worship in the faith of the Protestant Church.

Apollos fitted quickly into the ways of colonial Boston. John Coney the silversmith took the young immigrant for his apprentice. That meant that the lad would serve him and live in his house on Ann Street and be taught his trade. Apollos donned a leather apron and learned to hammer out spoons and porringers, to wrestle and pitch quoits with the other apprentices round Dock Square. The boys got up early and worked as long as daylight lasted. In the evenings they roamed the crooked streets and went swimming from the wharves. Some ran away, only to limp home hungry and receive a whipping. Others set fires and stole wigs and dallied with their masters' daughters. But not Apollos, nor his neighbor, the printer's apprentice, young Ben Franklin, nor Tom Hancock, who was learning the bookseller's trade and starting to build the fortune he would leave to his nephew, the famous John.

Apollos worked hard and prospered. When his master died he paid the widow forty pounds for his freedom. He set up his own shop and took a wife. He changed his French name to its English form—Paul Revere.

Deborah Hitchborn, wife to the first Paul Revere and mother of the second, lived on Ann Street too, in her father's mansion near Hitchborn's Wharf. She came of a sturdy rebellious New England family. One of her ancestors was forced to wear an iron collar round his neck, punishment for some forgotten crime. Another defied Governor Endicott and received a slap that set his ears ringing. Deborah's husband took a house for her near the fine home of Colonel Hutchinson, and they attended the Cockerel Church, so called because of the 172-pound brass bird on its weathervane. Here their first child Deborah was baptized, and later their first son on New Year's Day, 1735. They named him Paul.

The Revere children grew up in a Boston of narrow crooked streets that wound uphill and down, between overhanging wooden gables. The town was almost an island, connected with the mainland by a rough cart road over the mud flats of the Neck. The houses had garden plots behind them, and pens for the pigs and chickens that escaped sometimes and roamed through the heaps of offal in every gutter. Paul and his brothers caught eels in Mill Cove where the North Station now stands. His sisters gathered blueberries on the Common, which was still used as a cow pasture. Tall steeples rose up, and smoking chimneys, and the air smelled of salt and fish and tar and newly distilled rum. Mansions like the Hutchinson place stood close beside the squalid cottages and tenements that housed the poor. But the town's life centered around the wharves facing Boston Harbor and the brass cannon on Castle Island. And beyond lay the open sea roads that led out to all the world.

There was always the excitement of ships being loaded with pipe staves, saltfish, leather goods, horses, and cattle; of other ships bringing back sugar, rice, wine, furniture, and fine fashions. Busy folk darted everywhere, like waterbugs across a quiet pool: chimney sweeps, fishmongers, porters, shipwrights, smiths, weavers, merchants in gold lace, and clerks carrying ledgers. Paul grew used to the sight of them before he could toddle across his father's threshold. He grew used to the mingled sounds of Boston: the creak of a ship's windlass; the ring of hammers and the thump of wooden machinery; the great, swinging bells of the churches; and always the gulls crying on the blue air.

It was as a bellringer that Paul first entered history, not at his own church either, but at Christ's Church, later to be known as the Old North Church. Its steeple could be seen from the hills beyond the Charles River, and its eight bells were said to make the sweetest music in North America. Puritan Boston did not celebrate Christmas, but Christ's Church did. The neighborhood children loved to creep inside it and smell the Christmas greens that festooned its severely beautiful white walls and carvings. When Paul was in his middle teens he and a group of his fellows signed an agreement to serve here as bellringers and haul on the thick dusty ropes for at least two hours every week.

By this time he had left the North Writing School in Love Lane and gone to work in his father's shop where he slowly became a better craftsman than his father. We do not know how Paul looked as a young man, but we have a portrait of him painted by his friend, the artist John Singleton Copley, some years later. Dark-eyed and sturdy he looks, with a half smile on his face, and strong wrists and hands. He wears a plain white shirt with flowing sleeves and a simple waistcoat of blue. When men sang his praises in the street they called him "Bold Revere." Others spoke of him as steady, vigorous, and persevering. He was well-liked by many different kinds of men. He possessed the mixture of dashing courage and sober common sense for which young Americans are now famous all over the world.

When Paul was nineteen his father died, leaving no great estate but "a good name and seven children." Paul and his brother Thomas took charge of the Revere shop in Fish Street and went on making silverware.

A year and a half later the elder brother enlisted to fight against the French. England and France were still engaged in a series of wars that had begun before the Revere boys were born, and it was not yet decided which nation should rule most of North America. Paul went as a second lieutenant of artillery. His monthly salary was five pounds, six shillings, and eight pence. He took his own gun and powder horn, and the colony gave him a bullet pouch, knapsack, and wooden bottle. He wore a hatchet at his belt, and trousers either red or blue.

The American troops made little headway that summer against the better-trained French and their Indian allies. Paul and his comrades were stationed at Fort William Henry and spent their time felling trees and building whaleboats to carry the colonial troops across the lakes and into Canada. But they never crossed the lakes. Tormented by sickness, black flies, and scalping parties, the Massachusetts men rejoiced when November came and they were ordered home.

Paul did not enlist again but settled down in the shop on Fish Street. He married Sarah Orne, and within the year children began to arrive. For the next few years he busied himself with raising a family and making silverware that still exists, prized heirlooms of a later generation. Medals, spoons, thimbles; chocolate and coffee pots; massive flagons and christening bowls for the churches—no object was too big or too little for his careful workmanship. His finest silver belongs to the period of his young manhood, before the Revolution. He made humbler articles, too—tortoise shell buttons, branding irons, squirrel chains, engraved dog collars, even false teeth.

In the hard times of 1765 when money was scarce he learned to do copperplate engraving. He also tried his hand at political cartoons and verses. He helped to arrange for the first street lamps in Boston. Sometimes he served as clerk of the market. It was the clerk's task to take charge of the weekly open-air sales when the country folk drove into town with their produce. Paul's stalwart figure moved here and there among the oxcarts. His smiling ruddy face turned its appraising glance on baskets of apples, eggs, and turnips, crates of live fowl, and haunches of venison.

As time went on Paul took an active part in the growing quarrel between England and her American colonies. After the last war with France, England needed to raise money to pay her debts, and she felt that the colonies should help. After all, the war had been fought partly for their protection. Customs officers tried to enforce the Navigation Acts, to restrict trade and collect duties. But the Americans, used to trading freely as they pleased, resisted this move against what they considered their just liberties.

England's answer was to pass the Stamp Act. This act provided that the colonists must buy stamps and affix them to newspapers, legal documents, and playing cards. Stamp masters were appointed and set up offices to sell the stamps. Andrew Oliver, brother-in-law of Paul's rich and unpopular neighbor, Lieutenant Governor Hutchinson, became stamp master for Boston.

Swiftly now, the colonists all up and down the Atlantic coastline separated themselves into two parties. The Tories were for the most part wealthy men who favored England and wished to live under her rule as they had always done. The Whigs resented her attempts to control them more strictly and sought to carry on their affairs as free from English interference as possible. The Whigs, later known as the Patriots, were a more varied group than the Tories. Largely made up of craftsmen and laborers, they included also such Harvard-bred gentlemen as Dr. Joseph Warren, Paul's especial friend. Among them, too, was the fiery patriot James Otis, already showing signs of madness; talkative, out-at-elbows Sam Adams and his cousin John, the thrifty lawyer from Braintree; John Hancock, the rich merchant, noted for his fine clothing. Not only in Boston but throughout the colonies, the Whigs organized the Sons of Liberty, an inner group of brave men, eager to take action against the new laws so hated by the people.

Paul was an ardent Son of Liberty. Sometimes at sunset he would leave an apprentice to put out the charcoal fire in the brick furnace and sift the gold and silver dust from the floor sweepings. Then he would join his friends at the Salutation, the Green Dragon, or the Bunch of Grapes, taverns whose attics and back rooms provided secret meeting places. Over their grog and cider the Sons planned ways to move against English authority, and by the summer of 1765 they were ready.

One day in August a scarecrow-like figure of the stamp master was hanged from a huge elm near Frog Lane and Newbury Street. This elm came to be known as the "Liberty Tree," and soon every colony had a tree named for it. At dusk an orderly group of citizens cut down the figure and carried it away, chanting, "Liberty, property, and no stamps!" Later a mob entered Mr. Oliver's house, drank his wine, broke his windows, and threw him into a fit of terror.

They did even worse harm at the Hutchinson house two weeks later. Paul must have watched them attack the house of his Tory neighbor. Perhaps he even played a part, catcalled and swung an axe with the rest of them. They slashed carpets, broke clocks and chinaware, and carried away plate and jewels. They flung Thomas Hutchinson's priceless manuscript history of Massachusetts into the gutter. They tore down the fences and ruined the garden, but they did not harm the family. While the Sons of Liberty seemed to behave like a disorderly mob, they were really well-disciplined and acting under secret orders.

Unable to sell the stamps and enforce this law, England soon repealed it. In its place came the Townshend Acts, which put a tax on tea, glass, lead, and paper. Boston men resisted these acts so severely that many of the Tories withdrew to Castle Island, and in the fall of 1768 two regiments of British troops arrived to keep the King's peace in Boston. The effect of their coming was just the opposite, for the people rebelled against this highhanded measure. Redcoated troopers swaggered insolently about, enraging the citizens. The citizens teased and insulted the troopers.

Finally in March, 1770, an open street fight broke out; it was called the "Boston Massacre." A detachment of "lobster-backs" fired on the crowd that was heckling them. Before order could be restored, three persons were killed, two mortally wounded, and six injured. Paul stood in the shadow of the Old State House and watched the Boston Massacre. Later he made a pen-and-ink sketch of it that was used at the trial of the soldiers involved.

The British regiments were withdrawn soon afterward, and most of the Townshend Acts repealed, except for the tax on tea. Gradually, in spite of Sam Adams's effort to keep the rebellion alive, Boston began to quiet down. Most people got used to the tea tax and paid it with less grumbling. Then England made another attempt to enforce her authority.

In 1773 Parliament passed the Tea Act, designed to help the East India Company, whose warehouses were overstocked with that fragrant product so necessary in the daily lives of our ancestors. This act provided that only the company's tea could be sold in America, and that only duly appointed agents could sell it. The Tory Hutchinsons and their friends got themselves appointed as agents.

Boston men had been used to buying their tea from whom they pleased, and they intended to keep on doing so. But in their hearts was a new uneasiness. If England could interfere with the sale of tea, why not with the sale of molasses, or wine, or salt—or any goods whatsoever? They ordered the agents to go to the Liberty Tree and resign their commissions. Instead the agents retreated to Castle Island and prepared to carry out their work from the safety of the fort. As November drew to an end, all Boston waited tensely for the next tea ship to arrive.

Paul Revere had things other than the tea ships on his mind that autumn, for the past three years had brought him sorrow and happiness and many changes. A month before the Boston Massacre he had purchased a peak-roofed house on North Square and moved his family into it. In May, 1773, Sarah died, and in September he married Rachel Walker, whom he called his "dear girl"—Rachel, who would bear her own family and bring up his motherless children. And in this year, too, Paul bought his own horse and took off on his first ride in history.

The tea ships arrived—three of them—late in November. Next morning Paul mounted his horse and rode off to inform the surrounding towns of the arrival. We do not know what route he took or what village greens woke to activity at the sound of his voice in the crisp autumn air. But at last he was "booted and spurred and ready to ride." The great war for American freedom was about to begin.

"This meeting can do nothing more to save America," said Sam Adams.

He closed his mouth tight and looked around him at the Patriots gathered in the Old South Meeting House. All through the rainy December day they had waited to hear how Governor Hutchinson would dispose of the tea. Now the word had come that he refused to let the ships leave the harbor unless they first unloaded their cargo. But the Sons of Liberty were determined they should not unload their cargo.

In a moment Paul Revere, Josiah Quincy, John Hancock, and a score of others were on their feet. Their faces looked tense and grim in the candlelight.

"To Griffin's Wharf!" shouted a voice from the gallery.

Swiftly they scattered to their homes to prepare for the night's work. In the street some six thousand excited men and women cheered and went trailing after.

Minutes later a mob of wild-looking fellows swarmed across Griffin's Wharf to accost the startled captains of the tea ships. They wore rough clothes, shawls, and blankets. Their faces were smeared with mud, grease, and lampblack, and they muttered in harsh, disguised voices. Of course, they could have been Indians come down from the back country, but this man sounded a little like Paul Revere, and that man used a phrase heard often on the lips of John Hancock. In a few minutes they were busily at work bringing the tea chests up from the hold and splitting them open. Soon a heap of crushed, fragrant leaves floated on the icy salt waters of Boston Harbor. Then another heap went drifting away. By daybreak a long windrow of tea leaves swayed back and forth on the heaving tide all the way to Dorchester.

Tired but exultant, the raiders marched by fife music back to the State House. The British admiral watched them from a window.

"Well, boys," he called, "you've had a fine Indian caper. You've fiddled, but mind, you must pay the piper yet, boys!"

The Boston Sons of Liberty knew that he spoke the truth, but they did not care. They trudged back to their homes to shake the tea out of their shoes and wash their faces before their wild looks frightened the children.

Paul Revere mounted his horse again and rode off to carry the news of the Boston Tea Party to the Patriots in New York and Philadelphia. Most folk approved of what Boston had done, but when Benjamin Franklin in London heard of it, he was shocked and worried. Cautious John Adams shook his head. But his cousin Sam grinned broadly.

In the spring General Gage landed with eleven regiments to take over the government of Massachusetts and close the port of Boston. All the church bells tolled for hours after his arrival. With the port closed it seemed likely that grass would grow in King Street and all the people starve to death. Food and fuel became hard to get, and all the shops stood closed and shuttered. British regulars lodged themselves in the homes of reluctant citizens and set up an encampment on the Common.

The other colonies at once sent messages of sympathy and encouragement, also money and provisions. They were drawing closer together now, realizing that a blow against one of them was a blow against all. About a year after the Tea Party, Paul Revere rode north over the frozen roads to Portsmouth to warn New Hampshire that Gage meant to capture their small river fort and steal their military supplies. Within twenty-four hours the New Hampshire men rose up, took the fort themselves, and carried the stores away to safety in the back country.

This act of rebellion enraged the British, particularly King George. After that, Paul was a marked man. He could no longer ride freely out of Boston over the Neck, for the British would have stopped him. So he kept a boat hidden in the reeds of the Charles River. A man could always go fishing, couldn't he?

Spring came early to Massachusetts in 1775. By Saturday, the fifteenth of April, the fruit trees were in bloom and the fields already plowed. Late on that day an unusual stir could be noticed among the British troops in Boston. Something was afoot, and gossip quickly reported it to Paul Revere and his fellows, to Dr. Joseph Warren, the only Patriot leader left in town. General Gage intended to send troops to capture the colonists' military stores at Concord.

Before daylight on Sunday morning Paul got out his hidden boat and rowed over the Charles. Borrowing a horse, he set off to warn Samuel Adams and John Hancock, who were staying in Lexington. He may have kept on to Concord, for the town received a warning on that day. Its men and boys began at once to disguise the cannon and hide powder kegs and sacks of bullets. On his way home Paul stopped in Charlestown at the house of his friend, William Conant. He told Conant that when the British set out he would have lanterns hung in the tall steeple of the North Church to alert the countryside. One lantern would mean that they had chosen to march over the Neck; two lanterns, that they intended to advance by sea.

Then he went back to his house for supper—bread and cheese and a mug of cider, maybe—a kiss from his wife, and a romp with his children. He would try to get some sleep that night, since on the following nights he expected but little.

All day Monday the excitement mounted. On Tuesday the man-of-war, *Somerset* moved into the mouth of the river where its guns could command the route to Charlestown. Late in the evening the redcoats gathered at the foot of the Common and filed on board the waiting barges.

"By sea! By sea!"

The secret was out now. Joseph Warren had arranged for two messengers to carry the word to Adams and Hancock, and now he sent them on their way. William Dawes, a light-hearted young leatherworker who had fooled the British many times before, galloped over the Neck, got past the sentry, and took the long way round. Paul hurried over the cobblestones to rout out Robert Newman, sexton of Christ's Church, who had promised to hang the lanterns, but Newman was already in the street awaiting him. Soon the sexton and his vestryman, John Pulling, had their feet on the narrow wooden stair treads and were toiling upward. For years many people believed that the lanterns were hung as a signal to Paul, but this was not true. They were hung to alert the countryside in case he was killed or captured before he could reach the Charlestown shore.

Paul went home for a short coat and riding boots, but he forgot to take his spurs and some cloth to muffle the sound of his oars as they grated against the rowlocks and dipped and splashed in the water. His dog followed him unnoticed to a shadowy lane where he met two friends, Joshua Bentley and Thomas Richardson, who were waiting to row him across. They pointed out the mistake he had made, and Paul sent the dog home to Rachel with a note tied to its collar. The dog returned shortly with the spurs.

His friends led him to the house of a girl they knew, and she tossed down her petticoat from a gabled window. This they used to wrap about the oars and muffle them. A few minutes later the three men were out on the moonlight tide, row-ing swiftly, silently, past the *Somerset*. Just before eleven o'clock Paul stepped ashore in Charlestown. At the Conant house a group of his friends awaited him with a fine horse loaned by a rich man, John Larkin. We know little about this animal, but most New England horses of that time were small and sturdy, either dun, brown, or bay in color. Color did not matter to Paul, only speed, sure-footedness and endurance. Lexington was twelve miles away, and Concord six miles be-yond that. He thanked his friends and said good-bye to them. He swung into the saddle and rode off.

The road led over a dreary strip of salt marshes and clay pits fringed with scrub oak. Before he had gone far, two British officers challenged him, but he veered sharply toward the river and came out on another road leading to Medford. At Medford he awakened the captain of the Minutemen, and after that he alarmed every farmhouse all the way to Lex-ington.

"The Regulars are out!"

"The British are coming!"

Women scurried about trying to hide their children and family treasures. Men snatched their muskets and powder horns and took off after the rider.

It was close to midnight when Paul rode into Lexington. The moon shone down on the white church steeple and cast long shadows across the green. From Buckman's Tavern came a murmur of voices, the clink of glass against glass. Captain Parker and his Minutemen had gathered there to wait for the news from Boston. Sergeant Munroe and seven men stood guard about the parsonage where John Hancock and Samuel Adams had "retired, but not to sleep."

Paul rapped on the door and asked to be admitted. The sergeant reproved him for making too much noise.

"Noise!" shouted the enraged Patriot. "You'll have noise enough before long! The Regulars are out."

The Reverend Mr. Clark thrust his head from an upper window, but he did not recognize the man who stood in the shadows below him.

"We'll admit no strangers here at this time of night," he announced, "unless we know who they are and what they want of us."

But John Hancock had heard the voice and knew its owner. "Come in, Revere," he called. "We are not afraid of you."

Paul entered the parsonage and hastily told them that he with his own eyes had seen some thousand light troops take ship out of Boston and head in this direction. If reports were true, they sought not only to take possession of the stores in Concord, but to capture the rebel leaders as well.

John Hancock tore off his fine silk nightcap and called for his sword, saying he would march with the militia and fight in the ranks against this act of tyranny. Adams tried to dissuade him. They could best serve their country, he said, by protecting their own lives, since they were due to appear shortly at the Second Continental Congress in Philadelphia. While they were arguing, William Dawes rode in.

The two riders ate and drank together. It was not really necessary that they ride to Concord, for the town had been warned on Sunday and would have its supplies hidden. Moreover, the whole countryside was pretty well up in arms and ready to meet the British. But they decided to cover the last six miles if possible and carry the news to any Minutemen who had not heard it. A little way out of town they met young Dr. Samuel Prescott, who was on his way home from courting his girl, and Prescott joined them.

They had ridden about half the distance to Concord when a group of British officers blocked the roadway. Dr. Prescott urged his horse over a low stone wall and rode off, the only one of the three to reach his destination. Dawes made a dash for freedom, but reined his horse so short he fell off and the frightened animal escaped him. The Regulars pressed round Paul, pointing their pistols at his head, cursing him for a damned rebel. Paul flung their taunts back at them.

"Do as you please," he told the major who threatened to blow his brains out.

The officers conferred together and then started to lead Paul's horse back to Lexington, his bold rider still astride him. As they neared the town they heard a gunshot. Then another. Then a burst of firing. Had the battle begun? Again the officers hesitated. Then they ordered Paul to dismount, took his horse, and rode away. He stood all alone, there on the Concord road that ran straight between two stone walls in the chilly moonlight.

After a moment or two he made his way back, zigzagging across the fields and groping among the ancient stones in the Lexington graveyard. He found Hancock and Adams leaving the parsonage to take shelter at Woburn, and he accompanied them for a little way to ensure their safety. Then he and John Lowell, Hancock's clerk, returned to Buckman's Tavern to rescue the Hancock trunk and its contents of private and public papers. While they were engaged in this mission, the long lines of scarlet-coated British drew up to the green and faced the grim ranks of the Minutemen in their leather breeches and hunting shirts. The shot was fired. Guns smoked. Men lay fallen and bleeding.

But Paul's task was to rescue the trunk, and he went stubbornly about it. History loses sight of him just as he and Lowell carried their precious burden into the parsonage. It is likely that they stayed there to guard it or delivered it immediately to its owner. There is no record that Paul joined the men who fought at Concord Bridge or helped to hound the British back to Boston in the retreat that followed after. The adventure that was to make him famous was over. But he still had many services to perform for his country.

After the Battle of Lexington he served the colony as an express rider for about a month, earning five shillings a day. Then the Provincial Congress sitting in Watertown summoned him there and engaged him to engrave copper plates and print money to pay the expenses of the war and government. Paul succeeded in getting his family out of British-held Boston, and they lived in the country with other Sons of Liberty all around them.

After the Battle of Bunker Hill he had the painful task of identifying the body of his friend, Joseph Warren. He made the identification by the two false teeth he had fixed in Warren's mouth early that spring.

The British left Boston in 1776, and Paul returned there and was made a lieutenant colonel in the regiment raised to defend the city. Put in charge of Castle Island, he repaired the fort and its cannon. He accompanied the two expeditions that failed to drive the redcoat garrison out of Newport, and went to Worcester to receive the British and Hessian prisoners after the Battle of Bennington.

In 1779 Paul took part in an unlucky expedition to the

Penobscot River to attack British warships that had nested there to harass American shipping. The colonial troops were ill-trained, many of the officers inefficient and jealous of each other. Finally the enemy burned the ships that had brought Paul and his men northward, so they had to walk home, through the forests of what is now Maine and the seacoast villages of New Hampshire. Charges were brought against him for cowardice, disobedience, and unsoldierly behavior. He was relieved of his commission and went back to his shop in Dock Square.

This insult to his courage and loyalty made him angry. But it must have been good to feel the sleek touch of silver under his hands again, to live in his own house and enjoy his growing family. He found time to correspond with his Rivoire cousins abroad and exchange political views. A court-martial later cleared him of the ridiculous charges, but by that time the war was over. The colonies had won their independence. Paul found himself living in a free country.

For a time he ran a small shop near the Liberty Tree and sold fine fabrics, paper, pencils, sealing wax, wallpaper, playing cards, and spectacles. He had an artist's eye for the colorful wallpapers and described them for his customers—"tan orange on green"; "wheat blue on stone"; "rose blue on olive." During the war he had learned foundry techniques from the French forge master Louis Ansart, and now he set up a small forge near the familiar wharves of the North End. Here he produced copper and brass fittings for the ships of the new navy.

He turned also to the casting of bells. His first task of this kind was to recast the bell of the Cockerel Church where he had been baptized so many years before. He became nearly as famous for his bells as for his silver, and his metal business grew so rapidly that he set up a rolling mill at Canton and even went there to live for a time.

His real home after 1800 was a three-story brick house on the corner of Charter and Hanover streets, with rich furniture and spacious rooms. All his enterprises prospered, and he and Rachel enjoyed life here until her death in 1813. Paul missed her deeply, but five of his children survived—he had had sixteen of them—and he found himself knee-deep in grandchildren.

A new country was growing up, a new government and a new Boston. There are some signs that Paul clung lovingly to the old, but he never ceased to move forward and participate in the new. When British warships threatened his native city in 1814, the old patriot, now in his eightieth year, volunteered to help defend her just as eagerly as he had done half a century before.

Paul Revere died on a Sunday—the tenth of May, 1818—when all over New England his deep-throated church bells were ringing. He had performed many services for his country and won fame as a skillful artist and craftsman. But he will always be remembered for his cry in the darkness, "The Regulars are out! The British are coming!"—for his daring ride toward Concord under the April moon.

Chapter 6

———◆———

JOHN HANCOCK

While Paul Revere was playing his boyhood games on the streets of Boston's North End, two other boys whom he would come to know well in later life played much the same games on the green of North Braintree village, a few miles away. One was chubby John Adams, a farmer's son, and the other was frail, thin-faced Johnny Hancock, son of the minister. John Hancock was born January 23, 1737, to John Hancock II and the former widow Mary Hawke Thaxter. The Hancocks lived in a ramshackle parsonage where snow drifted under the door in the wintertime and the ink froze in the minister's inkwell while he was penning his sermons. Young John knew the feel of threadbare homespun clothing rough against his skin. He was more used to the taste of Indian cornmeal mush than the savor of fresh meat.

But Johnny had grand relatives, and visits to their homes showed him there could be an easier, more pleasant way of life. His grandfather, also a minister, also a John, lived on the ancient family farm in Lexington, home of the Hancocks for nearly a hundred years. And rich Uncle Thomas dwelt in a mansion on Boston Common that must have seemed like a royal palace to the poor little country boy whenever he visited there. Fat Aunt Lydia fed him sugar cakes, and her bluff, kindly husband filled his pockets with shillings. They had never a child of their own, and they made Johnny welcome whenever he could come.

When he was seven years old his father died. The other Hancock children, Mary and Ebeneezer, stayed with their mother. But Uncle Thomas sent the family coach to fetch Johnny back to Boston to be his adopted son.

The house that would be John Hancock's home for the rest of his life was built of granite with a tiled gambrel roof topped by a wooden railing that connected a pair of finger-like brick chimneys. It was reached by a dozen steps that led up to a wide doorway under a balcony. Inside the door a vast hallway ran straight through to a flower garden at the back. Here grew many strange plants brought home by the Hancock sea captains—apricot, nectarine, and mulberry trees. The great parlor had mahogany furniture and damask curtains and tall shining brass candlesticks to give light. The grand staircase curved upward toward the bedrooms with their carved four-poster beds. Behind the house stood the barn and the coach house. Before it lay the famous Common. All around rose up the roofs and steeples of Boston, and from the upper windows one could see the blue waters of the harbor, the small wharves and shops familiar to Paul Revere.

Young Johnny did not go to school the first year. He was too busy enjoying himself and being petted by his new parents. He got fine new clothes exactly like his uncle's, coats of lilac and green and peachbloom satin with embroidery and ruffles. Rich, colorful costumes always delighted him, and later he came to be known for them throughout the colonies. In 1745

he entered the Public Latin School where he remained for
five years, studying Greek, Latin, and penmanship. At the
age of thirteen he was ready for Harvard.

Aunt Lydia and Uncle Thomas drove him to Cambridge
in the new scarlet-lined chariot from London, taking the long
road over the Neck. Aunt Lydia's huge bulk might have put
too much strain on the unseaworthy ferryboat.

Once enrolled at the college the young prince of the Hancock family entered on still another way of life. All the students' names were posted on the wall of the "buttery hatch,"
a refreshment room. Their names were ranged in the order
of their social standing, and John ranked very high. This entitled him to a front seat and one of the best study chambers,
but he had to work just as hard as the boys whose names were
lower down. They got up early for six o'clock chapel, with
a scripture reading in Latin or Greek. Then came classes,
breakfast, more classes; then the midday meal, a pound of
meat and vegetables. Recreation lasted till two, followed by
an afternoon and evening of close study with a light supper
in between. As a freshman John had to do chores for the upper classmen—taking wigs to be curled and fetching food and
drink from the taverns. He studied the classics and divinity,
later physics, metaphysics, ethics, and religion. In his last
year he was allowed to relax with geography, geometry, as-
tronomy, and music.

Just what sort of a young man was John Hancock, whose
full purse later provided the money that made the Revolution possible? He has been described as shy, proud, sensitive,
"of a peevish temper which he had from his father." Others
said that he was a "respectable, good-mannered lad, obedient
to his superiors and a faithful scholar in school." But this was

a gay and riotous time at Harvard, a time of practical joking
and merrymaking in taverns. There is evidence that John
played the good fellow like the rest of his schoolmates, no
more and no less. All his life he never carried anything to ex-
tremes but always chose a middle-of-the-road course. In 1754
at the age of seventeen he took his degree and rode in the
family chariot back to Beacon Hill.

For the next ten years John lived the life of a young man
about Boston. By day he worked as a clerk in his uncle's prosperous importing house, The Bible and Three Crowns.
Thomas had started out as a bookbinder and bookseller. Later
he began to import all sorts of goods: hemp, lemons, Newcas-
tle coals, Cheshire cheese, Lisbon salt, tea, cloth, paper, glass,
French and Spanish wine. But his most profitable trade was in
whale oil and in furnishing supplies to the British troops in
America during the French and Indian War. John kept accounts, wrote letters, and tried to learn his uncle's successful
methods.

At night he often dined out, at the London Coffee House,
Luke Vardy's, or the Bunch of Grapes, and shared trade gossip with his fellow merchants. There were sports and good
times, too: riding, hunting in the country, sailing on the bay,
dancing, and lecture-going. The girls and the young men
strolled together in the summer evenings on the Common.
John made a dashing figure with his finely cut aristocratic
face, his splendid costumes, and his tall willowy figure. He
spent a year in London, where he learned about the English
side of the business and gained social polish. In 1764 Uncle
Thomas died and John inherited The Bible and Three
Crowns and some 80,000 pounds of personal fortune, sharing
on good terms with Aunt Lydia.

Becoming a rich man did not change his habits greatly. He continued to be a steady, punctual man of business. That business had grown to such a size that it was said more than a thousand families depended on Mr. Hancock for their daily bread. But earnestly as he applied himself, The Bible and Three Crowns never throve under John as it had done under Thomas. He never understood as well how to take advantage of changing conditions—and besides, he had other interests.

When the Stamp Act riots broke out he felt disturbed and uncertain if he could approve of such violence. But he liked the act no better than the rest of Boston and swore that one hundred guineas would not tempt him to apply for a stamp. Sam Adams talked persuasively to him, and a little later he was supplying money to aid the Sons of Liberty in their resistance movement. He had chosen the popular side, and the next year Boston chose him as one of its four representatives to General Court. His natural charity and kindness added to his popularity. When poor folks' houses burned down or sacks of firewood were needed in a hard winter, none was more ready to help than John Hancock. When Sam Adams got into money trouble, John helped him out of it.

In the spring of 1768 he had one of the King's inspectors hustled from the deck of his brig, the *Lydia*. A little later another of Hancock's ships, the *Liberty,* was accused of smuggling wine and seized by a crew of British marines. In return the Boston mob dragged one of the customs officer's boats to the Common and burned it in front of Hancock's house.

Arrested on suspicion of smuggling and for evading British taxes, John hired his old playmate, John Adams, as his lawyer and was let off for lack of evidence. As the colonies moved nearer to war Boston recognized the leadership of Hancock and voted him into more and more positions of trust. Although he lost a good deal of profit by it, he rigidly refused to import British goods except in those times when nonimportation broke down everywhere. Then he joined the other merchants and imported freely, being no more adverse to a bit of smuggling than his fellows were. After all, this, too, was in the interests of American freedom. Not always in agreement with the other patriot leaders, stubborn John Adams and his smooth-talking cousin Sam, he worked as loyally as they for the ideals more and more of the colonists were coming to believe in. Sam was poor and plain, a born agitator. John Adams was plain, thrifty, and cautious. But while Hancock kept his personal pride and love of display, he was always for reason and common sense, for talking matters over in search of a peaceful solution.

About this time he presented a fire engine to Boston, but insisted that his name should be placed upon it and that whenever a fire started he should have first call upon its services. He bought a concert hall from which British soldiers were excluded and gave money for the erection of a new Brattle Street Church, including its bell. With Paul Revere he served on a committee to provide Boston's first street-lights—three hundred of the latest white globes imported from England.

When the tea ships came into port in late November, 1773, Hancock refused to lead the meeting that was held in protest. But before the same meeting was over he declared that he would be willing to spend his fortune and his life if need be in such a cause. Whether or not he actually attended the Boston Tea Party is uncertain, but he helped to plan it, and old men who remembered it insisted that he was there.

The next March, though his feet were painfully swollen with gout, he delivered a stirring speech on the anniversary of the Boston Massacre. But more difficult labors were soon to be expected of him. In October two hundred and fifty representatives from all parts of Massachusetts gathered to form the First Provincial Congress, and they chose John Hancock to be their president. This congress soon voted to call up twelve thousand volunteers, the Minutemen. About this time rumors went forth that the King had ordered some half dozen patriots including John Hancock to be seized and beheaded. These brave men ignored the rumors and went about their business as usual. They had plenty to do. Times were growing hard in Boston, with the port closed, trade shut off, provisions scarce, and British soldiers everywhere.

These soldiers sang a song heard for the first time in America, a song that later became very popular here, but not the way they sang it.

> Yankee Doodle come to town
>   For to buy a firelock,
> We will tar and feather him,
>   And so we will John Hancock.

John himself answered by giving one of his most famous speeches. At a meeting in the North End somebody made the suggestion that it might be necessary to burn Boston in order to get the British out of it. No one else in town would lose as much if this should happen, yet he could arise and say, "Burn Boston and make John Hancock a beggar if the public good requires it."

For several years now John had been courting Dorothy—or Dolly—Quincy, a pretty young woman whose family's country place was close to his own childhood home in North Braintree. He must have visited her there, for even now we can see his famous script cut with a diamond ring on the narrow windowpanes. "Dear Cutte [Cutie?] you I love and you alone." Aunt Lydia approved of Dolly, her social graces and respectable family, and often invited the girl to pay long visits to the great Hancock house beside the Common. Dolly was inclined to be coy and hang back and look around a bit before she settled her mind to John.

In April of 1775 the Provincial Congress met in Concord. John, together with Sam Adams, stayed at his grandfather's old house in nearby Lexington, then the home of the Clarke family. Aunt Lydia and Dolly joined him there. The four guests were all in their beds that moonlit night when Paul Revere galloped up with the news that the British were coming. Soon the church bells began to ring, and some one hundred and fifty farmers and Minutemen assembled. John pleaded to join them, but Sam reminded him that fighting was not their business. They must save themselves, for they were shortly due at the Second Continental Congress in Philadelphia. So they slipped away to the safety of the lonely farms in Woburn and Billerica.

Dolly and Aunt Lydia were not wanted by the King. Being in no danger they stayed behind and helped the Clarkes to carry their valuables into the cellar. Then they watched the battle from the front windows. Later in the day they received a message from John. He wanted them to join him and bring along the fine large salmon that had been intended for supper. This they did and cooked it well for him in his refuge. John and Dolly quarreled, but Aunt Lydia saw to it that they made up again.

Shortly after this adventure John and Sam Adams started for Philadelphia. Other delegates joined them along the way, and they passed through New York and New Jersey in a triumphal procession. When they entered Philadelphia great crowds came out to cheer them, and all the bells set up a mighty ringing.

Philadelphia, largest city in the colonies, had cobbled streets lined with solid red brick houses. It was prosperous and stately, proud of its own culture. But its inns and byways were thronged with less fashionable folk: Indians in dirty blankets, Swedes from the Delaware, hearty Dutchmen, and hunters from the frontier carrying six-foot rifles. Its leaders, however, were the wealthy merchants in their silks and velvets and the cautious, more soberly clad Quakers. These men often looked down their noses at Boston's riotous behavior and the dangerous "leveling" ideas of Sam Adams. They were not yet quite ready to agree with him that one man was as good as any other man. But it was here in this conservative capital that the new government, the first real democracy, would grow.

On May 24 the Congress unanimously elected John Hancock its president. This proved to be a difficult office, for the new body had no real power and could not raise money or call up troops. Moreover the delegates disagreed violently, each one trying to further the interests of his own colony at the expense of the others. And here it was that Hancock showed one of his greatest strengths. He was able to get men to talk things over and come to peaceful agreement with one another.

Back in Boston his business had gone from bad to worse without its owner's guiding hand. His great house had been taken over by the British as headquarters for their officers. Up in Fairfield, Connecticut, Dolly was flirting with a young galant named Aaron Burr. But these reports troubled John far less than the disappointment he suffered when George Washington of Virginia was chosen to be chief of the Continental Army.

Never a soldier himself, he had always longed to be one and had once led a dashing troup of cadets that paraded proudly through peacetime Boston. Somehow he had hoped that his popularity and his many services to the cause would win him the commandership. It hurt him deeply that the Adamses had supported Washington rather than himself. He offered to serve as a private in the ranks, doubtless hoping to be appointed a staff officer. Washington politely evaded him.

Criticized by some for making haste too slowly, Hancock went on with the work of trying to organize the Congress. One last plea they sent to King George—the Olive Branch Petition —but the King would not so much as look at it. Clearly nothing was left now but to work for complete independence. Congress recessed in August. John Hancock donned a new crimson velvet coat and went up to Fairfield to marry his Dolly.

"That these United Colonies are and of right ought to be, free and independents states; that they are absolved from all allegiance to the British Crown and that all connection between them and the State of Great Britain ought to be totally dissolved."

Richard Henry Lee of Virginia uttered the words, but they were already in the hearts of many of his fellow members of of the Continental Congress that hot June day of 1776.

A general murmur of approval went round the room. John Adams seconded. Debate followed, and adjournment. President Hancock appointed a committee consisting of Thomas Jefferson, Ben Franklin, John Adams, Roger Sherman, and Robert R. Livingston to draw up a Declaration of Independence that should embody Lee's words. Then he turned resolutely to other affairs threatening his country. General Howe had moved out of Boston and was about to attack New York.

On July 1 Congress met again for debate and voting. At two o'clock on the afternoon of July 4 the Declaration was reported out of committee to the House with a recommendation for its approval. Quickly it was ratified. John Hancock, the president, signed it with a flourish. Until the other delegates signed a month later the whole responsibility for the Declaration was his. One man stood alone against the British empire!

He was to sign again, the official or engrossed copy, when the other delegates signed. This was the ceremony which was formerly supposed to have occurred on July 4, but it actually occurred on August 2. In front of the president stood a plain mahogany table with a silver inkstand and the plumes of several quill pens curving upward. The delegates sat ranged about the room in a semicircle.

Hancock stood up, grasped the pen, and wrote swiftly in his firm, beautiful script.

"There," he cried. "John Bull can read my name without spectacles and may now double the five hundred pounds upon my head! That is my defiance!" He paused and then added more soberly, "We must be unanimous; there must be no pulling different ways; we must all hang together."

"Either that or hang separately," Ben Franklin is said to have muttered. Whether he did or not, we shall never know.

Early in 1777 John Hancock's eyes were turning backward toward his native Massachusetts. The presidency of the Congress was a thankless task, no money, no real authority, all the delegates arguing with each other. Time after time he had given generously of his own funds to supply the tattered army. Time after time he had been rewarded with criticism and insult. Perhaps it was time to see if some other man could do the job better. He suffered a severe disappointment when the frigate *Hancock,* in whose construction he had taken so much pride, was captured by the British. Congress fled to Baltimore and then to Lancaster before Howe's advancing troops. No more could he refresh himself by entertaining his friends with wine and good dinners at his comfortable boardinghouse in Philadelphia. No longer could he bask in the comfort of Dolly's companionship. His courage and faith were as strong as ever, but his endurance began to wear thin.

On October 15 he asked for a leave of absence to restore his health and tend to his private affairs. At once he received permission to stay away until the first of the year. Sensitive as always and quick to take offense, it dismayed him that Congress should grant his request so readily. Were his services of so little account? Could they be so easily dispensed with? At his request Washington detailed an escort of dragoons to ride over the roads with him and see him home. Fortunately he was well away from Philadelphia before his fellow Massachusetts delegates voted against a measure to render him the thanks of his country. They did not do this out of petty jealousy, but they felt that "King Hancock" deserved no more special thanks than any other patriot. John would not have understood them. His old friendship with the Adamses seemed completely at an end. In some ways he remained an aristocrat who could not yield to their stubborn democracy.

Back in Boston, John busied himself by repairing his house on Beacon Hill and building a new banqueting hall. It had not been damaged as badly as some houses had been. Perhaps the British did not wish to stir up the people by harming the possessions of such a well-loved hero. He visited the taverns and markets, chatting with rich and poor alike, eager to maintain his popularity. When he returned to Congress the next June it was as a plain delegate, no longer its president. The chief business now on hand was the ratification of the Articles of Confederation that would set up the new government. When this act seemed certain of passage he went back to Boston and had a brief chance to follow one of his favorite dreams.

He had long held a rather empty title as major general of militia. Massachusetts troops were now joining in an attempt to throw the British out of Newport, and as Hancock had always fancied himself a soldier, he went along. The whole success of the campaign depended upon the support of the French fleet, and they, scattered by a storm and trapped by fog, failed to play their expected part. The venture collapsed miserably. Hancock hastened home. Some people criticized him for behaving vaingloriously in camp and quitting the battle ahead of his troops. But at least he arrived in Boston in time to soothe the wounded feelings of the leader of the French fleet. Admiral D'Estaing had put into port for repairs, and he also was suffering from criticism for his failure off Newport. This was a small chore, perhaps, but an important one. It was not a time when we could afford to make enemies of our French allies.

Dolly invited the French officers to the Hancock mansion for a grand breakfast. It was so well attended that it seemed to the people of Boston that the whole Common glittered with the gold lace of their uniforms. In fact so many guests appeared that she had to send to her neighbors to borrow whatever cakes they had on hand. A guard hurried forth to milk all the cows pastured on the Common in order to furnish drink. One young midshipman drank seventeen cups of tea. Others picked or ruined all the fruit in the garden.

John found himself happy now that he was at home again. And there was much to do to set up the new state government. In 1780 he was elected the first governor of the new Commonwealth of Massachusetts by a large majority. The war had gone badly in this year, but even worse was the situation caused by the rise in prices due to the constant printing of bad paper money. In Boston beef cost $8 a pound, sugar $10, butter $12, and tea $90. Corn sold for $150 a bushel, flour for $1575 a barrel. Sam Adams paid $2000 for a suit of clothes. This made life almost impossible for the poor and hard for everybody, including men as rich as Hancock. But even in these sad times the people did not begrudge him his pomp and ceremony. It brought color to their otherwise dull lives. They liked to see their hero do things with an air and a flourish. They loved him because he could remain an aristocrat himself and still not advance his own class at the expense of ordinary folk.

Sometimes he was guilty of petty tyranny, as when he reprimanded Paul Revere for letting the fort fall into disrepair during the time he commanded it. Many thought Paul had done as well as he could, considering the little money and few troops allowed him. But for the most part Hancock governed wisely. Except for a two-year interval he remained in office from 1780 until his death.

With the British defeat at Yorktown in 1781 the long war finally ended. The miracle had happened. The tiny, straggling colonies had defeated a mighty nation. John Hancock made no official response to the thrilling news. He was a sick man, tortured by gout and nervous trouble. He had grown bent and old before his time. He sent to England for a new stone-yellow coach lined with crimson velvet, painted with a coat of arms he is said to have designed himself. But most of the time he could not ride forth in the new coach. He ordered a silver tea service and some pewter plates for his dining room —pewter because the clatter of chinaware disturbed him.

But when Lafayette visited the city he provided sumptuous entertainment for the popular French leader—a welcoming speech at Faneuil Hall and dinner at the Bunch of Grapes. Dancing followed, but the crippled governor could hardly have stepped out in even the slowest minuet. Early in 1785 he resigned the governorship because of his health, but the people promptly elected him to the Congress at Philadelphia. For almost a year the Congress waited for him until at last everyone realized that he would never be able to travel that far.

Public office in Boston opened up to John Hancock whenever he wanted it, and in 1787 he again became governor. The year before a group of poor farmers in the western part of the state had risen up under the leadership of one Daniel Shay. They rebelled against the new taxes and laws that made life a burden to the poor debtor. The rebellion had been put down, and many of those who had taken part in it remained in jail. Hancock added to his popularity by promising to pardon them and to help remove the conditions that had driven them to rebel. In his new term of office he fulfilled both promises.

And now, harassed and ailing, he was called upon to perform his last great service for his country.

A convention called in Philadelphia had been busy drawing up the great document we now know as the Constitution of the United States. But it could not become the law of the land until the states voted to ratify it. In January, 1788, two hundred and eighty delegates met at Dr. Belknap's church in Long Lane to see what action Massachusetts would take. Everyone knew that John Hancock's opinion carried more weight than that of any other man. Would he favor the Constitution and a strong central government? Or would he prefer that the power remain in the hands of the individual states? Many private conferences were held before the meeting. Men on both sides of the question poured their arguments into the governor's ears. No one knows how much political bargaining went on.

When the day came for Hancock to address the meeting, several young men carried him bodily from his coach and settled him in the chair of honor. There, gouty, wrapped in flannels and obviously suffering, he dragged himself to his feet and delivered his great speech that was to ensure Massachusetts' support for the new nation. He had doubts and anxieties, he told them, but he believed that this Constitution should be approved as the foundation for a federal government. He then proposed a series of amendments which later became the so-called Bill of Rights part of the great charter.

Not all the delegates were swayed by Hancock's eloquence. Sam Adams stood against ratification and won some support for his views. As one writer put it, "he almost overset the apple-cart." But when it came to a vote, Hancock's wisdom prevailed. Massachusetts by a narrow margin of nineteen votes ranged itself with the states that had already accepted the Constitution.

Some careful historians have insisted that Hancock did not write his speech or compose the amendments, but he certainly agreed to them and presented them. Without his powerful support the fate of the Constitution might have been a different story.

Good times were coming back to Massachusetts. The years of fighting, hardship, and British oppression had become a memory. Shipping flourished again, more widely than ever as the great China trade had already begun. The new country was struggling to its feet and about to elect its first President. Few men doubted that General George Washington would be chosen to the office. But who would serve as Vice President? That was not so certain. Many men favored John Adams, but he had been living abroad. Perhaps his life there had changed him, put him out of touch with American ways. Would not John Hancock be a better choice?

Hancock himself thought so, and traveled widely through New England trying to attract votes, but his health defeated him. He could not make the journey to New York to win the support of the middle states. Certainly he could not go bumping over the tortuous roads to Virginia and beyond. In the end he had to see the post filled by John Adams, his boyhood friend, in later years his opponent. Facing it with as good grace as possible, he continued to direct the affairs of Massachusetts, to help it adjust to its new condition of statehood in a united government.

One last incident marred his declining years. In 1789 the newly elected President set out on a tour of New England. He had expected to be received by Hancock as soon as he entered Boston, but Hancock did not meet him. Perhaps the governor felt too ill to venture forth, as his friends have said. Perhaps a misunderstanding occurred. Washington proceeded to a public house and coolly and correctly declined an invitation to dine at the Hancock mansion. Notes flew back and forth. Each man seemed to feel that he should have the dignity of receiving the other. Eventually Hancock gave up and hobbled to pay his respects to the President. The United States, he conceded, was greater, more deserving of honor, than any one commonwealth.

Four more years were left to Massachusetts' first governor to limp regularly to the State House and the Council Chamber, to carry on the duties of his office. Much of the time he undoubtedly spent lying in the great bedroom at the top of his house where he could look out over the world he had known and in which he had been so powerful.

West Boston and the North End . . . Charleston . . . Cambridge . . . the Colleges . . . the bridges over the Charles and Mystic Rivers . . . the south and west heights of Dorchester . . . the cultivated highlands of Brookline and the rugged hills of Milton . . . Braintree and its poor parsonage he had left so long ago . . . farms, fields, villages . . . upon the east the islands of the harbor . . . the fort at Castle William . . . the wide sea he had sailed across as a young man. He had made changes in that world, changes he could be proud of.

John Hancock died on October 8, 1793, and was carried by a fine procession to the Old Granary Burying Ground. Dolly mourned him, and so did the people of Boston. Aunt Lydia had long been gone and so had his two young children. He had done so much for his country, much that had passed unnoticed. But he would be chiefly remembered for the simple act of writing his name.

Chapter 7

JOHN ADAMS

John Adams, the first famous man in what was to be a famous American family, began his long and strenuous life on October 19, 1735, in a Braintree farmhouse beside the Plymouth road. His father was John Adams, farmer, selectman, descendant of the Pilgrims John and Priscilla Alden. His mother, Susannah Boylston, counted among her ancestors the well-known Dr. Zabdiel Boylston, who had helped to introduce the smallpox inoculation to America.

Young John and his two brothers roamed the nearby woods, salt meadows, and plowland. Very early in their lives they learned to do their share in the work of the farm, planting, haying, harvesting, cutting firewood, and caring for the livestock. On Sundays they went to the sturdy granite meetinghouse and tried to sit still through four-hour sermons. On weekdays they trudged up Penn Hill to the schoolhouse under a white oak tree. Sometimes John helped the teacher, Mrs. Belcher, to carry her corn to be ground. She would give him three coppers and tell him to buy land with them.

John was the eldest, and his father wanted him to go to Harvard and become a minister. That meant long hours of studying Latin, and one day the boy rebelled against it and asked to be given other work.

"Very well, John," said his father. "If you do not like Latin, perhaps you will like ditching better. Go dig a ditch around the meadow there."

It did not take John very long to learn that ditching was far harder work than Latin. By noontime his eyes were turning eagerly toward his books, but he held stubbornly to the choice he had made. All his life he would hate to admit it when he was wrong. Not until the end of the second day did he swallow his pride and ask permission to leave off tussling with the flinty soil and go back to grammar and vocabulary. He eventually became a fine Latin scholar and went on reading the classics in that tongue even after he became an old man.

During his last two years at the college he belonged to a group of young men who met to read "new writings," poetry, and drama. In these sessions John declaimed with such fiery eloquence that his friends told him he would make a better lawyer than a minister. In the early days of the colonies lawyers had been looked on with disfavor as troublemakers of doubtful honesty, but during John Adams's boyhood the legal profession struggled into a new prominence. Formerly the clergy had been the most respected class, but now they were having to make room for the lawyers and the merchants. When John took his degree from Harvard in 1755 he did not feel certain he wanted to be a lawyer, but he doubted very much if he wanted to be a minister. Always devout and pious, firm in his religious faith, he had little patience with church quarrels and theological hair-splitting. Fortunately an opportunity came to him to serve as a schoolmaster in the town of

Worcester, sixty miles to the west. Thither he rode eagerly, all in the space of one August day, happy to have a little time before he must seek out a pulpit as his family expected him to do.

As a schoolmaster varied matters required his attention, "sometimes paper, sometimes penknife, now arithmetic, now a ferrule, then ABC, then scoldings, then flattering, then thwacking." But he found the citizens of Worcester to be sociable, generous, hospitable people. One, lawyer Putnam, became his friend, and together the two men went hunting, drank cider, and argued about politics and religion. Already John Adams at nineteen had come to believe that one day the American colonies must "set up for themselves," unless Great Britain succeeded in dividing them.

At the end of his first year in Worcester he left off school-teaching and went into Mr. Putnam's office to study law. Two years later, qualified in his chosen profession, he returned to his father's house and began his practice in Braintree. He was also admitted to the Boston bar.

For the next few years the young man divided his time between the law and the work of the farm. Sometimes he would ride into Boston, exercising his lively imagination on the way. He could imagine himself back into the previous century and roam with the Indians through the swamps and mountains. He could fly in his dreams to the moon and the fixed stars, across the Atlantic to present a case at the court in Westminster Hall or debate before Parliament. Once arrived in town, his attention would be caught up by the busy scenes around the State House and the Common—chimney sweeps, sawyers, merchants, ladies, carts, horses, coaches, marketmen, sailors, and soldiers. At court he argued cases and dined afterward with his fellow lawyers, meeting the most important men in the colony, becoming known to them.

On other days John remained in Braintree, pruning apple trees, cleaning the spring, planting corn, potatoes, and onions, and carting gravel. Between times he helped his fellow townsmen to settle their legal problems. Braintree men had the reputation of going to law more often than any other folk in the colony, so John had plenty to do. He read and studied, smoked tobacco, squired the girls, and reproved himself in his diary for wasting time. In the same volume he called himself "vain, puffy, and conceited," constantly examined his motives and conduct, and admitted that vanity was his besetting sin. It would please him greatly, he confessed, if he could be sure of immortality in the memories of the worthy, but he saw little hope of achieving it. Proud, quick-tempered and sensitive, resentful of criticism, he began to be known also as industrious and full of practical common sense. His town chose him to be road surveyor and then selectman, as his father had been.

He had a strong urge to write and contributed thoughtful, pungent essays to the *Boston Gazette,* commenting on local politics though he remained aloof from them. His distant relative Samuel Adams headed the Caucus Club, a political organization that met in garrets and moved behind the scenes to manipulate the vote in Boston elections. Sam did not invite his country cousin to participate at this time. Perhaps he did not consider him important enough.

In the fall of 1764 John married Abigail Smith, daughter of the Weymouth minister. Abigail was a very unusual girl for her time, charming and feminine but well-educated, able to quote Plato and Shakespeare. Her neighbors thought she had married beneath her, but Abigail did not think so. All the rest of her life she was to love and honor her husband, to bring up their family and run the farm successfully during his many absences. The young couple settled down in a house close to John's birthplace; and they might have lived in Braintree all their lives in happy obscurity, but by the time they were six months wed came the news of the Stamp Act. The American colonists set out on the road to war, independence, and greatness. Of course, John Adams and his good companion Abigail went along.

John immediately sought to resist the act with every legal means he knew. He argued that Parliament had no legal right to tax the colonies, since the colonies had no legal representation in that body. He stood strongly opposed to the violence that wrecked the Hutchinson house, but a few years later he referred to the Boston Tea Party as "the most magnificent movement of all." When the time came for every man to take sides, there was no doubt as to John Adams's position. He would support his native country, the home of his father and his grandfather, and he had no sentimental love for England merely because he came of English stock. But, on the other hand, he mistrusted the mob and could not condone their excesses when he considered them wrong. John Adams could be a statesman when his country demanded it of him, but a politician never.

After the Boston Massacre he defended the British captain who was involved in it and got him off without punishment. Many people admired him for this act of sober, unprejudiced justice, and just before the trial began they chose him representative to General Court. He divided his time between Boston and Braintree now, and admitted that he had more business at the bar than any other man in the province. James Otis chided him for being interested in nothing save to get enough money to carry him smoothly through the world—an unfair accusation. True, young Adamses were being born, including John Quincy, who would make as great a name as his father. They must be housed and fed and their education provided for. But John Adams never put the needs of his family above the needs of his country. He only worked a little harder, wore his shabby suits a little longer, and strove with the aid of his wife to manage the Braintree acres as thriftily as possible.

In 1774 he traveled to Philadelphia with Samuel Cushing, Samuel Adams, and Robert Treat Paine to represent Massachusetts at the First Continental Congress. Never had he been out of New England before, and it shocked him to hear New Englanders and their ways criticized by the free-spoken men he met as he passed through New York. Nor was Philadelphia much more to his taste. "Philadelphia," he wrote home, "with all its trade, wealth, and regularity is not Boston." All his life he would yearn toward his native Braintree whenever he was away from it.

Put on a committee for drafting a bill of rights, he worked diligently in true Adams fashion, but he did not spend all his time in the conference chambers. Wining and dining and getting acquainted formed an important part of congressional activity then as now. And he was rubbing elbows with other men prominent in their respective colonies—Roger Sherman, Caesar Rodney, Edward Rutledge, John Dickinson, Peyton Randolph, John Jay, Patrick Henry, and George Washington. About a third of them were lawyers like himself.

His diary contained many entries like this:

Dined with Mr. Chew, chief justice of the Province, with all
the gentlemen from Virginia, Dr. Shippen, Mr. Tilghman, and
many others. We were shown into a grand entry and staircase,
and into an elegant and most magnificent chamber until dinner. The furniture was all rich. Turtle and every other thing,
flummery, jellies, sweetmeats of twenty sorts, trifles, whipped
syllabubs, floating islands, fools, etc., and then a dessert of
fruits, raisins, almonds, pears, and peaches. Wines most desir-
able and excellent. I drank madeira at a great rate and found
no inconvenience in it.

John Adams had come a long way from the farm boy who
thought that reading Ovid's *Art of Love* and playing back-
gammon were a waste of time. And yet, not so far, after all.
His sober Puritan conscience disapproved of such activities,
and he seldom indulged himself more than sparingly.

When the Second Continental Congress met in May, 1775,
war had already broken out. Blood had been spilled at Lexington, and Bunker Hill was only a month away. John Hancock, his old playmate and former client, now joined the
Massachusetts delegation. During that session Adams had his
first serious political quarrel, one of many that would shadow
his career. He and John Dickinson of Pennsylvania disagreed
violently, Adams being against any moves of peace toward
England, and Dickinson being for them. The Massachusetts
man wrote indiscreet letters home referring to the matter,
they fell into the wrong hands, became public, and he received severe criticism. But he went doggedly on, working to
establish the American navy, set up a foreign policy, and
direct the twenty-five committees of which he was chairman.

Instrumental in forcing the Declaration of Independence
through the House, he performed an equally important serv-

ice when he presented the name of Washington as leader of the Continental Army and saw the appointment carried through.

By the fall of 1777 John Adams found it necessary to give some attention to his own affairs in Boston and Braintree. He would retire from Congress, he thought, and devote himself to his farm, his legal practice, and his growing children. Surely after four years of hard and ill-paid service in setting up the Revolutionary government, he had earned the right to become again a private citizen.

For three weeks he did just that. Then he rode up to Portsmouth to argue a case and met John Langdon, newly arrived from Philadelphia. Langdon whispered to him that he, Adams, had been chosen to go on a mission to France. Adams could hardly believe him. But two months later he was outward-bound on the high seas, headed for Paris to replace Silas Deane as a member of Franklin's ministry there.

No spirit of adventure came alive in John Adams to lighten the tedious voyage. He went forth gloomily, fearful lest he be captured by British sailors and lodged in the Tower of London, doubtful if his mission would be a success. He took his ten-year-old son, John Quincy, and the two Adamses struggled with seasickness and the difficulties of learning the French language. Once arrived in Paris he found the business affairs of the American delegation at a standstill. Ben Franklin had been for some time the ranking minister, and Ben, an old man now, was inclined to take life with a philosophic ease, to cultivate pleasant social relations with the French and make haste slowly. He kept no accounts and no record books. He spent far too much, Adams thought, in luxurious living.

"Stay on and have a good time," Franklin counseled the

newcomer, believing it was their duty to establish good relations rather than to take aggressive action. But Adams could not appreciate the older man's mellow wisdom. Too energetic and conscientious to fit into what he considered a meaningless whirl of pleasure, he returned to America in August, 1779.

Braintree welcomed him back and immediately chose him as its representative to the convention that was trying to work out a new constitution for Massachusetts. But the new year found him again in France. This time he went with specific instructions to remain there and negotiate peace and commercial treaties with the British as soon as it became possible. Rumor had it that King and Parliament were nearly ready to put an end to the war that had taken so many disastrous turns for them. But no official move had been made, and the fighting still continued in the American south.

Now John Adams was forced to play a waiting game. He did it grudgingly, with none of Franklin's serene patience and resignation. One British diplomat described him as "the most ungracious man I ever met." The suave courtiers and jeweled ladies did not know what to make of the short, fat little lawyer with his plain clothes and abrupt manners. And John, while he did gain some insight into the emotional, quickly changing Latin temperament, could never find it congenial.

"The public buildings, and gardens, painting and sculpture, architecture and music of these cities have already filled many volumes," he wrote to Abigail. "But what is all this to me? I receive but little pleasure in beholding all these things because I cannot but consider them as bagatelles, introduced by time and luxury in exchange for the great qualities and manly virtues of the human heart. I cannot help suspecting that the more elegance the less virtue, in all times and countries. . . . I could fill volumes with descriptions of temples and palaces, paintings, sculptures, tapestries, porcelain, etc., but I could not do so without neglecting my duty."

On his arrival he tried to establish friendly relations with the French minister, Vergennes, but very early he took the man's measure. The minister and, in fact, the whole French nation, except for a few idealists, were less interested in helping the young nation to the westward than increasing its own strength and power against its old enemy, England. Unable to remain inactive while events moved to the stage where he could begin his work on the treaties, Adams turned into something of a busybody. He wrote articles about America for the French press. He wrote letters to members of Congress complaining about Franklin. He wrote to Vergennes urging that the French take a more active part in the war. Vergennes sent a stinging reply, pointing out that Adams had overstepped his authority. Franklin was the only minister authorized to treat with the French court. Meanwhile he attempted to have Adams recalled.

Thus discomforted and desperately eager to do something for his country that would justify his continued presence abroad, he set out for Holland to see if he could secure loans from the bankers of Leyden and Amsterdam. Here he was more successful. He got along well with the thrifty practical Dutch, and Congress appointed him to be minister to Holland. He visited all the leading cities and won not only sympathy for his country but respect for it. Holland recognized the United States as an independent nation. Dutch banks made Congress loan after loan until 1788.

In 1782 Adams returned to France to carry out his original mission. Yorktown had been fought and the British forces routed in America. England now sent representatives to Paris to work out a treaty with the Americans and a formal ending of the war. Franklin and John Jay were also appointed to aid Adams in the work, and Vergennes was quick, as always, to try to meddle and advance the interests of the French. Congress had instructed its representatives to make Vergennes a party to all their negotiations and do nothing without his approval. But Jay and Adams decided to ignore him completely, and Franklin finally joined them in evading this irksome restriction.

Adams's chief contribution to the treaty was to arrange provisions that made it more acceptable to the English, and also to insist that American fishing rights off the northeast coast be retained. Once the Americans had completed their work, they had to wait until France and England had arranged a separate peace, which was concluded in September, 1783.

Now, perhaps, John Adams could go home. His business affairs needed his attention. His salary was small and could ill support the style of living he was forced to maintain. Mrs. Adams, too, had to practice thrift. He felt that his children would be but poorly off, not so well left by their father as he was by his.

His hopes proved to be vain, however, for there was still the matter of the commercial treaty to be worked out. In 1784 his family joined him, and early in 1785 he was appointed ambassador to England.

When Abigail Adams and her daughter, young Abigail, were presented at the Court of St. James, they did not wear

Braintree homespun but expensive gowns made by the court's own dressmaker. King George kissed Mrs. Adams sedately on the left cheek, but the Queen showed obvious embarrassment, and the American lady admitted that she "had disagreeable feelings, too." On the whole the ceremony proved to be very disappointing, and the ladies of the court were in general "very plain, ill-shaped, and ugly."

The Adamses settled down in Grosvenor Square, where they soon found that everything cost too much. Tea and coffee proved too great a luxury for daily use. Silk stockings and stays had to be ordered from Paris. John could not bring over the wine cellar he had laid down at Auteuil without paying a duty on it. Instead he contented himself with the nut-brown English ale so praised in the old ballads. Officials, even earls and their ladies, paid their duty calls, but they did not come back and issued few invitations. The English aristocracy had decided to treat these representatives of an upstart rebel nation with cold civility. This did not matter to the Adamses. They made up their minds to endure their stay and to do what they had come there to do.

John Adams was charged less with fostering goodwill than with trying to protect American rights and see that indemnities were received for injuries suffered in the war. But he met with a delaying policy that even his energetic attempts could not outwit. England, he soon saw, was not likely to give up the chain of frontier forts she still occupied, and she was attempting to hinder American commerce in the West Indies.

About this time the Barbary pirates were attacking our ships in the Mediterranean, and though Adams sat down in London with the Sultan and smoked a pipe "over two yards long," matching him whiff for whiff, they came to no agreement. Jefferson, now minister to Paris, believed in taking strong action against the pirates, but Adams, more cautious, advised buying them off. The two men corresponded constantly during this period and were the greatest of friends, though differences had already begun to grow up between them. Jefferson distrusted the new Constitution when they received a copy of it. Adams felt highly enthusiastic. Jefferson trusted the common man and feared that the power of the President might become too great. Adams felt that the common man needed a benevolent authority to protect his freedom.

Jefferson came to visit him, and they toured Stratford on Avon and Pope's estate at Twickenham. But Adams found himself more interested in a new type of patent wheel made from bent timber than in literary shrines. John and Abigail went to English Braintree, but he expressed the doubt that any of his family ever came from there. They went, too, to Winchester, where Abigail, whose mother was a Quincy, proudly deciphered the signature of a Quincy on the Magna Carta, drawn up in 1215, the first document granting civil liberties to Englishmen. They visited Plymouth, too, and Oxford, but always found the English weather abominable.

John spent most of 1787 writing his truly great book, *Defense of the Constitutions of the United States of America*. He embodied in it all his political philosophy and all the political theories and philosophies that were in the minds of the Congress when they went about shaping the American nation. In it was the philosophy, too, that underlay most of the state constitutions.

Young Abigail was married in London to her father's aide, Colonel William Smith. John Quincy had chosen to return to Harvard and complete his studies rather than go directly into the diplomatic service as his father's secretary. With his family growing up and affairs at home needing his attention, his mission in London at a stalemate, John Adams tendered his resignation and sailed back to America.

The United States he returned to in 1788 was still a very young nation, not completely organized, not sure of itself. But it had entered upon a new prosperity. Trade flourished and fortunes were being made. Adventurous skippers had opened the sea routes to the Far East, bringing home exotic Oriental wares. Carpenters were hammering up mansions for them in all the seaport towns. New villages sprang up along the westward-running roads, and settlers' axes set the tree line back further every year. This seemed good in his eyes, but he felt more dubious about other changes. Many of the stanch old Revolutionary patriots had disappeared from the political scene. Their places were filled by younger men, less skillful and devoted, he thought, but shrewder in their pursuit of self-interest. He could not be sure how they would receive him, and he doubted their integrity.

But when he first came home from London, Massachusetts gave him a glorious welcome. He purchased a large house not far from the old Adams farm, with mahogany-paneled rooms to set off the elegant furniture he had bought in Paris and Holland. Here he arranged his best friends, his books— treatises on law and government, histories, translations and original texts of ancient writers. But he was not to remain among them long. He had a part to play on the national scene.

Perhaps the most misunderstood man in American history, John Adams believed firmly in a republican form of government. He believed it should have executive, legislative, and judicial branches, independent of each other, kept in order by a system of checks and balances. But he believed in a strong executive, and that made many people think he was a monarchist and would like to turn the president into a king and establish an American royalty. He was used to protocol and a certain dignity and ceremony in the conduct of government. This made him further misunderstood. And he did not really trust the ability of the common people as Jefferson did. He believed they should be governed by the intelligent, the well-educated, and the well-born. He believed the government should give the people, not necessarily what they wanted, but what was good for them. From Adams's time to the present the tide of American political thinking has all run the other way.

But his own theories of government underlay most of the state constitutions as well as the federal Constitution. He entered eagerly into the political game where he knew the rules, since he had helped to make them. He did not know that during the next decade the rules would change past his understanding.

The political parties in our modern sense were just emerging, and John Adams would never be a party man. His stubborn integrity led him to defy his friends when he considered them to be wrong. And this turned many of his friends into enemies. Even as early as this, Alexander Hamilton, the brilliant and dashing lawyer, financial genius, protégé of Washington, had begun to work against him. Adams was soon to quarrel with Jefferson and disagree with Washington himself. Jealous of the great general's popularity, he distrusted him as the scholar, the man of law, often distrusts the military man.

In the fall of 1788 the United States held its first national election. The carefully designed electoral system went into action slowly, with much creaking. As it operated in the beginning there was no candidate for Vice President and no party ticket. The man who received the most votes would be president; he who received the next highest number would succeed to the second highest office in the land.

No one doubted that Washington would be his country's choice for its first executive, and so he was, winning all sixty-nine electoral votes. Most people expected Adams to take second place, and he did, but with only thirty-four votes supporting him. Although no formal parties had as yet been organized, most men were divided in their thinking into two groups known as the "Federalists" and the "Anti-Federalists." The Federalists, originally so called because they had supported the new Constitution, were for the most part the wealthy, more influential citizens who believed themselves capable of taking a part in the new government. Opposed to them stood the embittered common people, disappointed because they had no part in the growing prosperity, because their lot had not improved as rapidly as they had expected it to. Many of them were not allowed to vote because they did not have the property qualifications the law insisted upon. Alexander Hamilton, acknowledged leader of the Federalists, lacked confidence in Adams and gave his followers the order to scatter their votes instead of uniting behind the man from Braintree.

As Vice President, John Adams had to preside over the

Senate, and he found this difficult because his office required
that he maintain neutrality in debate and only cast a vote in
case of a tie. Adams loved nothing better than expressing his
own opinion and boasted, "I have never sacrificed my judgment for kings, ministers or people, and I never will." When
he did have a chance to vote, he usually sided with the Federalists, not because he thought of himself as a Federalist,
but because he honestly agreed with their thinking in these
particular instances. He supported Hamilton's financial policy, and this pleased the younger man, so that he did not
oppose him when he was chosen Vice President for the second
time. However, Adams's political writings at this time,
springing out of his disapproval of the French Revolution,
displeased both Hamilton and Jefferson.

In 1796 Washington refused to run for a third term, and
Hamilton again tried to divert the vote from Adams, but
with only partial success. Adams won a clear victory and
became second President of the United States. The "Repub-
licans," as the Anti-Federalists were beginning to call themselves, supported Thomas Jefferson and swept him into the
Vice Presidency.

During the four years they served together, the old friends,
Adams and Jefferson, drew a little nearer together on some
points, but Hamilton remained "the Duke of Braintree's"
implacable foe. The main issue of John Adams's single term
as President was the controversy with France. The French
Republic, established after the Revolution, broke with the
United States. They refused to receive American envoys, and
war seemed likely to follow. Adams took a strong stand, saying, "I will never send another minister to France without
assurance that he will be received, respected and honored as

the representative of a great, free, powerful, independent nation." He advocated strengthening the navy to protect our shores in case of attack, but he did not close the door to further negotiations if the French wished to enter into them.

Hamilton and his followers, however, were eager for war. At their behest Congress passed the Alien and Sedition Acts, designed to keep French refugees and immigrants from entering American political activity. It established a navy department and a strong provisional army. To command this army Adams appointed Washington. Washington chose Hamilton, Pinckney, and Knox, in that order, to be his staff officers, and the Senate confirmed them. Adams insisted that the men should be ranked in reverse order, and he yielded only when Washington threatened to resign.

Word came now that the French were willing to confer and would welcome an envoy. Hamilton and his followers still preferred war, but without consulting them, Adams fearlessly appointed W. Vans Murray to attempt this mission. His own cabinet, dominated by Hamilton, sought desperately to prevent this move, but on the eve of the election in 1800 he completed the papers and ordered Murray to leave for the French court, knowing well what it would cost him.

Just before this decisive act that destroyed his political future, John Adams had brought Abigail from Quincy to the half-finished White House to be its first lady. She found the new city "pretty enough" and the official residence well located with a distant view of the river where white sails passed up and down. Only six rooms were ready to be lived in, but the size of the building and the activities to be carried on required a staff of thirty servants. It was a chilly autumn that year, and in spite of the forests that surrounded the new capital, the Adamses had trouble getting firewood. A great unfinished audience chamber had to be converted into a drying room where they could hang up the laundry. Perhaps Abigail did not mind that her stay here was not to be long.

If he had been willing to compromise and do some electioneering, Adams might have been granted a second term, for the Federalists were loath to go out of power. But he would not stoop to that. He had done as he saw fit, and he would stand on his record. When the votes were counted, Jefferson and Aaron Burr received seventy-three votes apiece, Adams only sixty-three. Sure of the past, but bewildered as to the future, he prepared to leave the new executive mansion having shivered through only one winter there. His last important act was to appoint John Marshall as Chief Justice of the United States, one of Adams's greatest services to his country. Few men could have interpreted and administered the Constitution better than this Virginia frontier lawyer was to do.

On Adams's last night in the White House he packed his books and papers. When morning dawned on March 4, 1801, he called for his coach and drove off into the spring mist— "five hundred miles through the bogs"—home to Braintree which had been renamed Quincy nearly ten years before. Perhaps he should have remained to welcome Jefferson and attend his inauguration. It would have been a gracious gesture. But John Adams was not given to gracious gestures when his heart was not in them. He would have considered it hypocrisy. Surely his old friend would understand.

A tremendous rainstorm greeted his return to Massachusetts, and the flooding creeks deposited a hundred loads of seaweed in his barnyard. All the better to fertilize his fields with, he thought. His old neighbors gave him a glorious welcome. John Adams had come back to his father's farmland, back to his books and his broad rooftree for the last time. Here he could supervise the work of the farm in the mornings, write and study in the afternoons, and enjoy the companionship of children and grandchildren. There would be plenty for him to do.

"The only consolation I shall want will be that of employment," he wrote to a friend. "Ennui, when it rains on a man in large drops, is worse than one of our northeast storms; but the labors of agriculture and the amusement of letters will shelter me. My greatest grief is that I cannot return to the bar. There I should forget in a moment that I was ever a member of Congress, a foreign minister, or President of the United States. But I cannot speak."

Friends urged him to write a defense of his administration, but he contented himself with a series of letters to the *Boston Patriot,* and he did not issue these until he had been out of office for some years.

The famous Dr. Rush of Philadelphia suggested that he write his memoirs, but he refused. What could he say, he replied to the doctor, that would set him apart from any other liberal New Englander. He had been a church-going animal for seventy-six years, from the cradle, and agreed that religion and virtue are the only foundations, not only of republicanism and all free governments, but of human society.

As he grew older he and Jefferson renewed their correspondence and took pleasure in recounting to each other how spry they were in spite of their years. Adams, past seventy-five, walked three or four miles every day and still rode occasionally, though rarely for more than ten or fifteen miles. Jefferson, some ten years younger, rode every day, and three or four times a year he traveled to Poplar Forest, some ninety miles off. Their letters steered away from touchy current problems, but discussed their deep-rooted philosophies more thoroughly than the two friends had ever been able to do before.

Abigail and two of his children having preceded him, John Adams felt little apprehension or desire to linger when he sensed that his last days were approaching. He had been weakening for some time, and on the morning of Independence Day, 1826, while the town prepared for its celebration, his doctor announced that the ninety-year-old patriarch could not live beyond sunset.

Still sitting upright in his chair, surrounded by grandchildren, John Adams struggled to utter his last words.

"Thomas Jefferson . . . still lives," he said.

He never knew that Thomas Jefferson had died at one o'clock on that very day.

If people misunderstood John Adams, he left them in no doubt about what he considered his greatest achievement. Long after the end of his political career, and not many years before his death, he wrote his own epitaph.

"I desire no other inscription over my gravestone than this: 'Here lies John Adams, who took upon himself the responsibility of the peace with France in 1800.' "

Chapter 8

--------⦿--------

ETHAN ALLEN

Ethan Allen is more to be dreaded than death with all its terrors. . . . His Followers or dependents are a collection of the most abandoned wretches who ever lived, to be bound by no Laws or Ties.

The boy bending over his books spread on the cabin floor had no thought that any such words as these would ever be spoken about him. If he had, his straight mouth would have curved in a smile and his bold eyes twinkled. He would have been amused and a little proud—perhaps delighted. But that time was not yet, not this March evening in 1754 when he had reached no nearer to manhood than the age of sixteen. Up in Cambridge John Hancock and John Adams were studying too, the harder lessons prescribed by Harvard College. By Dock Square Paul Revere worked late, hammering out his first designs in enduring silver. But Ethan Allen sprawled by the fireplace in his father's frontier log house and wrestled with grammar.

Bark still clung to the rough-hewn walls, and a tree stump rose from its roots in the center of the room to serve as a table. Here burned the one light, a tallow candle in a bat-

149

tered holder. All around, with little order possible because of the cramped space, spread the household goods of the Allen family: spinning wheel, benches, guns, axes, scythes, saddlebags, and powder horns. Crazy shelves held pewter plates, wooden bowls full of dried pumpkin, and stone jugs of cider. From the rafters hung cured hams, sprigs of cooking and medicinal herbs, and reddish brown braids of tobacco. Two smaller rooms held the beds, clothing, and few personal possessions, the whole overrun by dogs and children.

Ethan scowled and put his fingers in his ears for a moment. Then he rose, went to the door and opened it. The cool night air felt good to him after the smoky room with its clamor of voices. Soon the willow buds along the river would be opening. Soon he could go hunting in the deep woods, once the snow had thawed. It almost seemed to him that he could smell spring. He stood there looking out at his home town of Cornwall, Connecticut, on the Housatonic River, which gleamed in the dim light. Not that he had been born there, but he had lived there most of his life, and it seemed like home.

There had been Allens in New England ever since the three brothers, Samuel, Thomas, and Matthew, had come to Massachusetts with the Dorchester Company in 1632. Soon after, in search of greater freedom and more opportunity, they followed Thomas Hooker to western Connecticut. They were restless, energetic, hopeful, fathers of many children. They were shrewd traders and good hunters, outspoken, fearless, loving the woods. They liked to drive hard bargains and win wagers. Ethan's father Joseph married Mary Baker of Woodbury, and the couple made their first home in Litchfield. Here Ethan was born, January 10, 1738. Shortly afterward they bought a "right" in the new town of Cornwall and moved twenty miles northwest over the rolling green hills with the baby and a few cows.

By the time Ethan had grown old enough to take much notice of the town it had become a sizable cluster of log cabins huddled on a flat beside the river. It had a green, a tavern, a meetinghouse, stocks, and a whipping post, but no mill or roads that coaches and chaises could travel.

When Joseph needed to have his grain ground, he had his oldest son take it to Woodbury. Ethan, dressed in moccasins, deerskin hunting jacket and linsey-woolsey breeches, would lead the horse across the hills and long valleys, the grist swinging in saddlebags, his fowling piece on his shoulder, and his tomahawk ready. The boy made friends in Woodbury, for his uncle, Remember Baker, introduced him to the young men of the town, and then there was the miller's daughter, Mary Brownson. Mary was older than he, quiet, religious, delicate, with no gift of laughter. But she had a kind heart, and seemed drawn to the lively, eager frontier lad. She gave him cider and hasty pudding while he waited to receive his flour.

Standing in the cabin doorway now, Ethan thought of Mary. He wondered if his father would send him to Woodbury in a week or two. But his thoughts turned quickly from this pleasing prospect to another matter, a more disturbing one—the thing that had happened in the church last Sunday. Reverend Solomon Palmer, who had served for fourteen years as pious and respected minister of the parish, had suddenly risen in the pulpit and announced that he could no longer follow the Congregational Way, the way of most of the churches in New England. He had decided to become an Episcopalian!

Ethan, sitting in a front pew, was very much startled. Since then he had studied his Bible closely and questioningly. If Mr. Palmer had been wrong for so many years, then perhaps all the other ministers were wrong. It was up to him, Ethan Allen, to examine his own beliefs. Perhaps he, too, might choose to leave the Congregational Way. His father had been a selectman and a moderator of town meetings, but his father's ideas were not always orthodox. Perhaps that was why his father had arranged for him to be tutored by the Reverend Jonathan Lee, of Salisbury, so that he could go to college and study the truth and find out for himself.

Ethan sighed. Yes, college and learning would be well enough, but he felt more at home in the alder swamps, watching for deer signs, where they had trampled the grass at the drinking places or scraped their horns on the young green boughs. He could listen to lectures, no doubt, but he would rather listen for the sound of a beaver's flat tail as it thwacked the water to warn its dam-building comrades of his approach. He sighed again and turned back to his books. Choices were not always easy to make, boy or man.

But it turned out that Ethan had to make no choices. Within a short time his father was dead and buried in the pasture behind the cabin. The eldest son, with seven younger brothers and sisters to be responsible for, had to give up all thoughts of college and devote himself to plowing and raising cattle, getting the seed sown and the corn harvested and the firewood cut for winter. But he never gave up his studies entirely, or his questioning attitude toward religion.

He did leave home long enough to march to Lake George with a small company during the French and Indian War, but he spent only fourteen days in the service. On this trip he heard for the first time of the rich lands east of the Hudson and north of Connecticut, the wide fertile valleys and tall forests in a country that had no name. He must have thought of it often, but he did not go to look at it then.

He probably worked in some capacity at the large round Ore Hill in Salisbury, said to be filled with rich deposits of iron, for when he went into partnership with John Hazeltine and the Forbes brothers to operate a forge there, he contributed fifty-four pounds and "experience." The forge, built in 1762, the only one in Connecticut, was immediately successful. In the same year Ethan married Mary Brownson and took her to Salisbury. With the profits from the ore business and a shrewd manipulation of mortgages, land, and a little cash, he helped his brothers to get their start in life.

In Salisbury lived an itinerant doctor, Thomas Young, whom Ethan had known when he went there to be tutored, and now he spent much of his leisure time with this amateur philosopher, discussing books and ideas and drinking grog. Young was a rationalist and a skeptic, and made fun of old-fashioned Puritan theology. He introduced the younger man to the writings of Plutarch, Locke, Hobbes, Machiavelli, and some more questionable authors. But long before this, Ethan Allen had examined his own mind and become what many of his neighbors considered a blasphemer. He went about saying he did not believe in Original Sin, Christ, or Christianity, and he possessed a rich store of brimstone profanity which he was quick to use on all occasions.

Thomas Young left Salisbury shortly after the Allens settled there, but before he left, he wrote a pamphlet which interested Ethan greatly. It dealt with the land quarrel between the governors of New York and New Hampshire. Both of them had been granting land to settlers in the area between the two colonies, and trouble arose as the grants conflicted.

For the next few years the Allens lived fairly quietly, Ethan and Mary and his brother, Heman, in a square, clapboard house on a hill beside the mill brook. He went to court once, charged with illegally impounding his neighbors pigs for rooting in his garden, and won his case through his own arguments: brilliant, forceful, and profane. He also successfully defended himself for getting inoculated against the smallpox without the consent of the selectmen. He appeared in court for assaulting George Caldwell at a party held to celebrate their conclusion of a business deal. He bought more ore rights, and Heman opened a general store. Children were born to him, a daughter and a son, Joseph.

In 1765 the Allens moved to Northampton where Ethan was to be part owner and overseer of a lead mine. But the lead mine did not prosper. Creditors sued. Moreover the townspeople disliked Ethan's scoffing attitude toward religion. They resented his making fun of their great religious leader of an earlier day, Jonathan Edwards, who was still revered locally. Eventually the selectmen requested him to leave town.

This happened in the summer of 1767. Mary and the children went back to live with Heman in rooms over the general store in Salisbury. Ethan followed his heart and turned, as the men in his family had always done, to the frontier. The Stamp Act had come and gone. Troubled men in the New England seacoast towns were preparing for new attacks upon their rights and liberties. But Ethan Allen was not among them. He knew, he thought, where to look for freedom. He went north to Bennington and spent all winter tramping on snowshoes through the New Hampshire grants, sleeping in trappers' cabins and living on venison, salt pork, and cornmeal. He crossed the Green Mountains and came down the Connecticut Valley in the springtime, home to his debts, his responsibilities, and the irksome restrictions of small community life. But he vowed to himself that he would soon be off again. It was here, between the Hudson and the Connecticut rivers that his future would lie.

There was surely plenty of quarrelling and excitement going on in that area of the New Hampshire grants about the time Ethan began his visits there, and excitement and quarreling always drew him. He returned again and again, spending only the coldest months of the winter with Mary and his growing family in Salisbury. He bought land in the north and sold it to his Connecticut neighbors. He made friends in Bennington, and Arlington, in Castleton and Poultney, little frontier towns between the forests and farmlands. The land he and his friends owned had all been granted to them by the New Hampshire governors, and now settlers from New York were moving in and trying to take it over. But by the Great Jehovah, they wouldn't succeed, not if his name was Ethan Allen!

In 1770 he was chosen by a group of the landowners to go to Albany to defend their rights to their purchases before the New York courts. He took a skillful lawyer with him, but in spite of this he lost the case. "Yorkers" were confirmed in their right to settle the disputed area.

But Ethan shook his head and thrust out his strong chin. "They will find," he announced, "that the God of the valleys is not the God of the hills."

"What do you mean?" inquired the bewildered lawyers.

"Come to Bennington and find out," answered Ethan truculently.

Back in Bennington himself, he gathered his friends together at Landlord Fay's Catamount Tavern and organized a group of stouthearted fellows who vowed to defend their land titles and not be at all squeamish about the way they did it. They chose Ethan to be colonel and Seth Warner and Remember Baker for lieutenants. When New York's Governor Colden heard about it, he announced scornfully that he would drive them into the Green Mountains, and from that they took the name they made famous in history, "the Green Mountain Boys."

We are used to thinking of the Green Mountain Boys as an organized Revolutionary War regiment, and eventually they did become that, but around the time of the Boston Tea Party they were a wild and boisterous group of frontier outlaws, terrorizing the hapless Yorkers, beating and insulting them and burning their houses down. And they declared themselves to be innocent of any wrongdoing. They were only protecting their property, they said, against the encroachment of strangers who had no right to be there.

Ethan himself was a tall, powerful man of massive strength, great stubbornness and daring. They said in Bennington that he could tell the best stories and mix the best drinks of any man who ever came to town. Singlehandedly he once beat up a New York sheriff and his posse of six men. On another occasion he picked up two of his opponents and cracked their skulls together. Once when a group of Regulars had him cornered in a tavern he succeeded in getting them so drunk they paid no attention when he slipped out the door. After the Green Mountain Boys made him their leader he put aside his hunting shirt and got himself a uniform with epaulets and much gold braid. He led his Boys on a series of raids and exploits that have become almost legendary. One of their practices was to set up a "Judgment Seat" under a tall pine tree, and after considering the case of their victim they would give him a flogging which they called the "Chastizement with the Twigs of the Wilderness."

He could wield a pen, too, as well as more savage weapons, and when the hard winter kept him indoors he used the time to write out laborious and misspelled articles for the Hartford weekly paper, defending the rights of the New Hampshire and Connecticut settlers. These articles were forthright and humorous and attracted many readers. The governor put a price on his head, but Ethan only laughed and continued to harass the arrivals from New York.

Several of his brothers had joined him, and Ira, the youngest, made a trip to the lands round the Onion River (now the Winooski), and urged Ethan to settle there. In 1772–73 the Allen brothers, Ethan, Ira, Heman, and Zimri, and their cousin, Remember Baker, organized the Onion River Company. They succeeded in getting control of some 45,000 acres and planned to build roads and a general store as the nucleus of a settlement. Ira surveyed the land, and Ethan began selling it off in small parcels to men who promised to bring their families there. But whenever he encountered any Yorkers trying to survey land he drove them off and smashed their surveying instruments.

The Boys never let business keep them from fighting. They attacked and routed the settlers of Durham, and Ethan produced a pamphlet about his private war with New York Colony. He went around the frozen countryside in a sleigh, selling copies of it and talking about the cause to anyone who would listen—also praising the richness of land on the Onion River. Ethan was, among other things, a promoter, a speculator, and a salesman. Rough and crude when he wanted to be, he could be slick as maple syrup when he felt such behavior was more likely to get him what he wanted.

As Ethan traveled from town to town hawking his pamphlets, he could not help but see that a larger war than his own was in the making. Howe's redcoats held Boston and involved themselves in constant brawls with the people. Up in Portsmouth the New Hampshire men had seized the King's fort and prepared to oust their Tory governor. Every village and crossroads was divided into two camps, its Tories and its Sons of Liberty, and a man had to make it plain to his fellows just where he stood. Ethan liked nothing better than to make his opinions plain.

"Ever since I arrived at manhood," he later wrote, "and acquainted myself with the general history of mankind, I have felt a sincere passion for liberty. The history of nations, doomed to perpetual slavery, in consequence of yielding up to tyrants their natural-born liberties, I read with a sort of philosophical horror."

When he heard the news of the Concord fight his blood was up, and he rode quickly to Bennington. He found the principal men of the countryside gathered there to see what action they would take, and before long he had engaged himself to lead his Green Mountain Boys in an attack on Fort Ticonderoga. This stone fortress, half in ruins now, had been built in 1755 to protect the narrow strait that joined Lake George and Lake Champlain. Whoever held it held control of the important inland route to Canada. It was now garrisoned by only a small company of British Regulars, but Ethan realized that this outpost of the enemy could mean trouble for his nearby Onion River land. For more reasons than one, he saw, Fort Ticonderoga had to be taken.

Brother Heman came in about that time, very much of the same mind. He had just been in Hartford where he had recommended to the Committee of Correspondence that steps be taken to try and gain control of Lake Champlain. A certain militia captain, Benedict Arnold, had recently told them the same thing, and advised them to seize the guns of the British garrison at Fort Ticonderoga. They sent Heman north to arouse the Green Mountain Boys to aid in this venture.

It did not take the Boys long to go into action. They chose Edward Mott as chairman of their "board of war" and Ethan Allen their field commander. The place of rendezvous was Hand's Cove on the eastern shore of Lake Champlain, close to the fort, but hidden from it, and all through the mild spring night men came pouring in. Ethan busied himself posting sentries and going over the plan of attack with the other officers. The waning moon cast little light among the shadowy trees where no campfires burned, and no torches. The lake stretched westward, black and quiet. No stir of lights spoke of alarm in the sleeping garrison. In an hour or so . . .

Toward morning a proud-faced, scarlet-coated captain arrived with his servant and introduced himself. He was Benedict Arnold, he said, and was commissioned by the Cambridge Committee of Safety to enlist four hundred men to attack Ticonderoga. If Ethan would just step aside, he would take over command of the Green Mountain Boys and bring the affair to a speedy conclusion.

The Boys jeered and protested. They had been promised they could choose their own officers, and they had chosen Ethan. They would fight under him, or they would go home.

Finally the officers worked out a compromise, and Allen and Arnold marched together at the head of the expedition. About two hundred men had assembled, but the two boats at their command would hold only eighty-five. Those lucky enough to get aboard landed at Willow Point where Ethan called for a vote of confidence, every man who was for going forward to lift his gun. High into the air went every weapon —rifles, bunderbusses, fowling pieces, even clubs.

Then they surged ahead over a crumbling wall and through a wicket gate with Ethan in the lead. A startled sentry fired once and then fled into the depths of the fort to give the alarm. With cheers and Indian war whoops the Americans followed. Ethan ordered them to form in a hollow square, but they felt too sure of success to bother with discipline and hastened to overrun passageways, guardroom, and bastions. One soldier thrust out a bayonet, but Ethan thwacked him over the head with the flat of his sword and called for their commander.

Now a half-dressed officer with his breeches in his hand appeared at the top of a stairway and cried out, "By whose order do you enter His Majesty's fort?"

"In the name of the Great Jehovah and the Continental Congress," shouted Ethan Allen.

After that it was soon over. Commander Delaplace, seeing

he could do nothing else, stepped out and surrendered his sword, while the Green Mountain Boys rounded up the rest of the garrison.

Captain Arnold seemed to feel himself more in sympathy with the British officers than with the unruly frontiersmen in their worn hunting shirts and tattered homespun. He tried to keep them from seizing whatever liquor, food, and clothing they could lay their hands on, but he did not succeed and the move made him unpopular. Ethan did not do much to restrain them, but he gave Delaplace a receipt for ninety gallons of rum taken from his private cellar, and later the King's officer collected payment from Connecticut Province. Riders were dispatched to Philadelphia and Albany to tell of the glorious victory, and the fort's colors were delivered to the Continental Congress, just gathering for its second session. Arnold kept trying to gain control, but the Green Mountain Boys and their allies from Massachusetts and Connecticut did not like Arnold. They scoffed and jeered and even took a shot at him when no one was looking. Five years later when he committed treason against his country, they probably shook their heads over their grog in the Catamount Tavern and muttered to each other, "We expected as much."

Ethan sent the prisoners to Connecticut with a letter to Governor Trumbull, "I make you a present of a Major, a Captain, and two Lieutenants in the Regular Establishment of George the Third." Then he turned his attention to what he believed must be done next. He went about trying to advance north across the lakes, to take and hold the whole region, but he received setbacks. More British Regulars arrived, and Arnold remained on the scene, annoying as a cloud of blackflies about the head when a man was trying to remain secret in a forest ambush. Sometimes his counsel was wise, but Ethan never considered it so.

And worst of all was the appalling message that arrived from the Continental Congress. Instead of praising him for the capture of this important fortress, they ordered him to remove the British cannon to the south end of Lake George where they could be restored to His Majesty's subjects when the now desired peace and harmony were brought about.

That was too much. Ethan sat down and wrote an angry letter, advising them that peace and harmony were no longer desired, that they should pursue the war of rebellion against tyranny as hotly as possible. Then he proposed a plan whereby he should be allowed to enlarge his forces and march into Canada.

But even more than a chance to go forth on this expedition, Ethan wanted to have his Green Mountain Boys recognized as a regular regiment in the Continental Army, and he and Seth Warner traveled to Philadelphia to try to bring this about.

A story is told that when they set off on this journey they stopped at Bennington and went to a church where Parson Dewey was offering a prayer of thanksgiving for the capture of Ticonderoga. In the midst of the service Ethan interrupted by calling out, "Parson Dewey, Parson Dewey! Please mention to the Lord about my being there!"

Parson Dewey opened his eyes and murmured, "Sit down, Ethan Allen. When I want you I will call upon you." Then he went on praying.

Ethan and Seth put up such good arguments before the Congress that it passed a resolution authorizing the regiment and granting them regular army pay for the Ticonderoga expedition. The men were to have the privilege of choosing their own officers, and Ethan presented a list of possible choices to the New York Provincial Congress. He no longer had any quarrel with them, since all hands had united now to save the country. He thought the men would be likely to want himself and Seth for field officers; Remember Baker, Robert Cochran, Peleg Sunderland, and Heman Allen as captains; Ira and Levi Allen as first lieutenant and adjutant; Elijah Babcock as commisary; and Jonas Fay the doctor and surgeon.

But when the committees from the various towns met at Cephas Kent's tavern in Dorset, they chose Seth Warner as lieutenant colonel and Samuel Stafford major. Heman and Levi Allen were voted commissions, but Ethan Allen received no office at all.

He felt bewildered and furious. Why had he been left out? Had he not done more than anyone else to organize the Boys? Did anyone doubt his courage or his leadership? Had his friend Seth Warner betrayed him, or had they voted for Seth because he was quieter and not such a rebel and a firebrand? He told himself that the committee members who cast the vote were older, less daring men, who distrusted him because he was not a regular churchgoer, because he was always setting off on some wild adventure. His Boys would still prefer him, he thought, and he was right in that. When General Schuyler came to Ticonderoga to prepare the troops for the march into Canada, so many refused to move without their old commander that he permitted Ethan to go along— provided he would behave himself and submit to orders. Bitterly as it hurt his pride, he agreed to Schuyler's terms. It was not the general he blamed, but the stiff-necked, ungrateful old men whose farms he had saved from the Yorkers not too many years ago.

As the expedition moved northward, Schuyler sent Ethan ahead with a small following. They were to try to persuade the French settlers to join the Americans. Ethan's well-known smooth talk should accomplish this. Also they were to purchase supplies and reconnoiter. Moving faster with every step as he advanced toward the enemy, again under his own authority, Ethan gathered a somewhat larger following, made up of some of the French and some of his old friends from the Connecticut militia.

On the morning of May 25 they attempted a rash and ill-planned attack on Montreal and were defeated. The end of the day found the favorite Green Mountain Boy in the hold of a British prison ship, attached with handcuffs and heavy leg-irons to a bar some eight feet long. General Prescott gloated and swore he would send the rebel to England to be hanged at Tyburn.

The prisoner's spirit remained unbroken. Once he used his powerful teeth to bite through the iron nails that held his handcuffs. The nails had to be replaced with a padlock. When the guards tormented him, he swore such mighty and original oaths that the ship's crew gathered to listen.

But oaths did not help him. He was sent to England for a brief period and then confined at Pendennis Castle near Falmouth. When sightseers from the town strolled out to take a look at the strange prisoner in his red worsted cap and fawn-skin jacket he would harangue them on the courage of his countrymen and the virtues of liberty. Not knowing what else to do, the authorities finally decided to return him to America. On the way back the ship stopped at Cork, and the citizens collected a boatful of gifts for the man who had dared to defy their old enemy, England. They included money, wine, chocolate, pickled beef, plump turkeys, two pairs of shoes, two beaver hats, and silk suits of blue and green. But the captain soon relieved him of most of these.

Back in New York he received his parole after a time, and was free to wander about Manhattan and live by his wits, while his brothers kept trying to arrange for his release. A fellow prisoner described him at that time as "a robust, large-framed man, worn down by confinement and hard fare—a suit of blue clothes with a gold-laced hat that had been presented to him by the gentlemen of Cork enabled him to make a very passable appearance as a rebel colonel." His style of speech was said to be a "singular compound of local barbarisms, scriptural phrases, and oriental wildness, ungrammatical, but forceful." About this time the British offered him a commission, high pay, and large future land grants if he would join them and help to conquer America. He refused them vehemently.

He was finally exchanged in May of 1778 and went at once to Valley Forge to report, then back to Salisbury. Here he found that Heman had died only the week before. His own son, Joseph, had also died while Ethan lay in a British prison, and this affected him deeply. Mary and the girls now lived in Sunderland, not far from Bennington, and he hastened there as quickly as possible.

The familiar countryside had not altered much during the years he had been away from it. The same cabins stood along the same muddy lanes, the same oxcarts trundled by, taking the grist to mill; children and dogs and pigs roamed through the village streets; the farmers plowed, and the women cooked and spun.

But in other ways he found great differences. While he was away the towns had banded together and drawn up a constitution, the first in all the colonies to outlaw slavery. They had elected a governor and a legislature and become the free and independent state of Vermont. His old friend, Thomas Young, suggested the name, taking it from the French phrase for "green mountains." Congress refused to recognize them, but they continued to organize their affairs, ignoring the refusal.

All this excited Ethan greatly. Washington sent him a brevet colonel's commission in the Continental Army, and this pleased him; but he was not ordered to a line regiment —perhaps because of his reputation for unruliness. Nor was he eager to go. He had much to do to make the state of Vermont a going concern, and he went swiftly about it.

As a prime mover in all the affairs of the new state, his first task, he decided, was to obtain money for necessary expenses. This he did by selling off the confiscated Tory estates. His next task was to get recognition from Congress. This, in spite of several trips to Philadelphia and much political conniving, he was unable to do.

Some sixteen New Hampshire towns along the Connecticut River wished to join Vermont, and Ethan promised not to accept these rebellious towns if the New Hampshire leaders would use their influence to get Congress to recognize his state. This plot did not succeed and made enemies for him when it was discovered. Later Washington promised recognition, but Congress repudiated his promise.

Ethan went doggedly on, managing his Onion River land, writing vehement articles and pamphlets defending his views, and renewing his war on the Yorkers. He held no civil office, but he was chosen brigadier general of the Vermont militia. Brother Ira served as treasurer, state surveyor, and member of the council. The Allen brothers' little office in Sunderland was in effect the state capitol. Ethan appeared before the legislatures of other colonies pleading their cause, carried on all sorts of business affairs for the state, and held it stubbornly together.

Denied by Congress again and again, partly because of the influence of New York, a few discontented souls in the tiny republic began to whisper among themselves that perhaps they should turn to Great Britain and ask if she would take them back under her protection. During the spring of 1780 Ethan's behavior became most erratic and peculiar. He was often absent from home with no excuse, said he was going one place and showed up in another. Rumor had it that he conferred with Sir Henry Clinton in New York, but this was disproven.

Indeed, his position during the last years of his life is uncertain, and there are two schools of thought about him. Undoubtedly he entered into negotiations with General Haldimand, commander of the British forces in Canada. He did discuss with him, thoroughly and over a long period, the possibility of Vermont's entering the British Empire as an independent unit. Some authorities feel that Ethan was serious in this and plotted a treason as great as Benedict Arnold's. On the other hand, he wrote over his own bold signature that he wanted "no part in any damned Arnold plot to sell my country and my own honor by betraying the trust reposed in me."

He also affirmed that once Congress was willing to accept Vermont as a member of the United States, he would cease all negotiations with any foreign power.

The quarrels with the Yorkers went on, making his later years as full of colorful and violent episodes as his youth had been. With the end of the war the real estate business improved and profits came in steadily from his Onion River property, though he frequently found himself land poor.

Mary died in 1783, and the next year he married Mrs. Frances Buchanan, a beautiful and spirited young widow who bore him three children, including a much-desired son. At this time, too, he completed and published a book called *Reason the Only Oracle of Man,* which described his philosophy and his since been known as "Ethan Allen's Bible." He believed in a world governed by the laws of nature; he denied Puritan theology and the doctrine of Original Sin. He insisted on freedom of the will, that every man could work out his own individual destiny.

The settlers in the Wyoming Valley, most of them natives of Connecticut, were having troubles similar to Vermont's. They wanted to remain an independent territory and not be forced to incorporate with Pennsylvania, and they sought Ethan's advice. He made two trips there to counsel them, and on his return set about building himself a house on a thousand-acre farm in Burlington. Here he removed his family in the fall of 1787.

But though he was barely fifty years old, Ethan's great strength had begun to fail him. One February day in 1789 he drove to the home of a friend in South Hero to buy a load of hay to get his livestock through the rest of the winter. Some of the old Green Mountain Boys joined them, and they sat late around the fire, drinking punch and telling stories of the old days when they had driven the Yorkers home howling for quarter. Perhaps they spoke, too, of the future that lay before Vermont, the state they had created with their own stubbornness and valor. Recognition would surely come, if not in their time. As Ethan's Negro servant was driving their oxcart homeward, he noticed that his master had fallen suddenly silent. He put out a hand to touch him, and realized that he was alone—alone except for the body of a man whose spirit had departed. Ethan had gone to his final home.

A story exists that he believed in the transmigration of souls—that after death men would be raised up again in the form of animals—and expected to live again as a great white horse. His old friends looked wistfully out sometimes, across the long valleys and rounded green hills, half-expecting to see a huge white stallion, mane streaming in the wind, hoofs pawing the well-loved Vermont earth. But Ethan never came.

Many men had more contacts with him than Washington had, and, yet, perhaps it was Washington who knew him best, out of his great genius for knowing men. Thus Washington wrote, "I have been happy in the exchange and a visit from Colonel Allen. His fortitude and firmness seem to have placed him out of reach of misfortune. There is an original something in him that commands admiration."

Without that fortitude and firmness, without that original something, there might never have been a state of Vermont.

Chapter 9

———————◦◦◦———————

JOHN STARK

Those of ye name are descended from one John Muirhead
. . . who at hunting in ye forest of Cumberland, one day seeing King James ye 4th . . . in hazard of his life by a bull hotly
pursued by ye hounds, stept in between ye King and ye bull,
and gripping ye bull by ye horns . . . almost tore ye head
from him . . . for which he was called STARK and his posterity
after him.

Whether John Stark, born in Londonderry in His Majesty's
Province of New Hampshire on August 28, 1728, was directly
descended from this stalwart knight of the fifteenth century
is uncertain. But he certainly bore the old name in the new
world with a great deal of credit, and stood always ready to
seize by ye horns and wrestle to earth any unwise bull that
rose against him.

John's father, Archibald, went out of Scotland as a very
young man, settled in Ulster, and learned the carpenter's
trade. He married one Eleanor Nichols and fathered several
children. In 1719 a group of hardy, adventurous folk left the
Irish lanes and villages and sailed for America to establish
a new township, first called "Nutfield" and then "London-

derry," a little to the southeast of the falls of the Merrimack River. With them went Eleanor's parents, James and Margaret Nichols, and the next year the Starks decided to follow. Tragedy rode the little ship, for smallpox struck in midvoyage and all the Stark children died. Unable to land in Boston because its people feared the pestilence, the captain finally found a haven for his passengers in the village of Sheepscott near what is now Wiscassett on the coast of Maine. Here Eleanor and Archibald Stark stepped ashore in the late autumn with winter coming on, far from the kindred they were seeking, childless as on the day of their marriage.

Nothing is known of their early years in America except that they survived them, and the first child of the new family, a daughter Anna, was born in Londonderry, probably at the home of her Nichols grandparents in 1722. Archibald worked as a carpenter, cleared his land some two miles south of the meetinghouse, and planted corn, beans, flax, and potatoes. He purchased farm animals as soon as he could afford them and shot wild game for the table. He never ran for town office, but his name appears on various documents as a thrifty and respected citizen. He also developed a profitable sideline by extracting and selling turpentine from the pitch pine trees that grew in the sandy soil around his clearing. Eleanor came of humble folk and made her mark rather than writing her name, but like all the Londonderry women she knew the secret of curing and weaving flax in the Irish way, and added to her household chores the production of fine linen. Two more children, William and Isabel, were born to them, and then John, who would live for almost a hundred years and see the birth of a new nation. John would, in fact, take ye bull by ye horns—ye British bull this time—and help to bring the new nation about.

Sometime in the spring of 1736 the Stark homestead burned to its stone foundations, and Archibald did not re-build it. Instead he sold the land, and later owners let it go back to a tangle of blackberry vines and Queen Anne's lace. He used the purchase price to take up a new grant at the Amoskeag Falls on the Merrimack, and here he built a sturdy house of native white pine that stands today, perched on its high bank above the busy industrial city of Manchester. Long rows of red brick mills and a nineteenth-century canal have intruded upon the landscape that held only the tiny frontier village of Derryfield, fields, and forests and fishing weirs in Archibald Stark's time. He built a sawmill, too, on the brook that flows out of Dorr's Pond, and here eight-year-old John began to learn the craft of the sawyer and lumberman that would support him for much of his lifetime.

Very little knowledge remains of what his parents were like, except for one anecdote that shows Archibald possessed a sly, teasing sense of humor and Eleanor had plenty of spirit. Once, according to legend, a party of Boston men visited the Stark home and peered into the south room where Eleanor did her spinning. Seeing her at her wheel they asked Archi-bald who this lovely creature might be. "Oh," he answered with a casual shrug, "that is but a girl I have got to do my work for me."

Quite understandably Eleanor jumped up, her eyes flash-ing, and gave him the edge of her tongue in broad Scots. "Ye lee! Ye lee, Archie Stark, ye know I'm your ain wife and as good as any o' ye!"

Young John learned, too, all the ways of country living, all the skills needful to men of his place and time: how to spear the salmon and net the shad from the swirling waters between the massive rocks; how to ride and trap and shoot and deal with Indians and travel the winter woods. He learned to live by the rhythm of the seasons that decreed the time for plowing, planting, and harvest; how to conduct himself by the stern moral code that insisted a man should deal justly and honestly with his neighbors, tighten his belt and live sparsely if need be. He could read and write and reason. Of book learning he had and needed but little.

So the boy grew up, practicing these skills and virtues till the first time he appears in history as an individual, not simply a member of his father's family. This was in 1752, and John Stark, twenty-three years old, steps forward for his initial role, thin, muscular, somewhat above medium height, with sharp, austere features, pale blue eyes, and a pale skin that could turn even paler with rage or resentment, never with fear.

As soon as the spring thaw melted the snow in the woods and set the ice floes tumbling down the rivers, John and his brother William, together with two other young men, David Stinson and Amos Eastman, ventured northward in search of beaver skins along the Baker River. They fell in with a party of St. Francis Indians, William escaped, Stinson was killed, and Eastman and John Stark were taken prisoner and carried farther north to the headquarters of the tribe. Rescued by a party of Massachusetts men, they returned home some two months later. Stark's redemption fee was $103 or, according to some accounts, an Indian pony. But perhaps his captors would have been willing to pay it themselves in order to be rid of such a troublesome character. When they gave him a hoe and sent him into the fields—this work was usually reserved for the squaws—he chopped down the shoots of young corn and carefully spared the weeds, thus ruining the season's crop. When they set him to run the gauntlet, down two lanes of braves armed with clubs who were supposed to beat him as he dashed through, he seized a club from the first attacker and continued on his course, thwacking the Indians soundly before they could thwack him. His pale eyes gleamed and his thin lips taunted, "I'll kiss all your women!"

This delighted the old men and they called him, "Young Chief." Though Stark fought later against the Indians, he was never an implacable enemy of the red man and often commended the Indian's moral virtues. He also reproved his comrades for scalping them indiscriminately in time of peace. But from this adventure he learned much about the Indians and their ways of fighting, knowledge that he put to good use later on.

With the outbreak of the French and Indian War, John Stark joined the Rangers, a company raised by one Richard Rogers. Rogers's father and Archibald Stark had taken up land in a new village west of the Merrimack, first called "Starkstown," and then "Dunbarton" after the Scottish home of the Stark family. Captain—later Major—Rogers was a young man with a large nose, a swaggering manner, and a bad record for counterfeiting, but always bold and plausible. He trusted John Stark and depended on him much of the time as second in command. The Rangers saw service on the Hudson, at Fort Edward, at Fort William Henry, and round Lake Champlain.

They were a brave and seasoned outfit, well suited to their task of scouting the enemy outposts and harrying the French and Indians. Rebellious and hard to control, they responded, if sometimes grudgingly, to the powerful will of John Stark. They fought under rigorous frontier conditions, suffered from cold and frostbite in winter, blackflies in summer, smallpox and lack of clothing at all times. Stark conducted himself well on numerous small missions and saved the day in several encounters.

When Lord Howe joined them at Fort William Henry on June 28, 1758, his coming swelled the assembly to 16,000 men. All through the next week the troops were gathering at the head of the lake. The sound of bugles, drums, and bagpipes broke the quiet of the wilderness rendezvous, and countless oars flashed in the bright water. Polished gun barrels and splendid uniforms gleamed amid the thickets of birch, pine, and fir, and craggy mountains lent majesty to the scene.

Having heard that he was knowledgeable in the ways of the enemy, Lord Howe sought a conference with John Stark, and the two men sat together on bearskins in an ordinary tent to discuss their prospects for the taking of Fort Ticonderoga, the objective in view. Servants brought them a simple meal, and they planned the strategy of attack. Some scouting parties reported that the French defenses could be easily overcome, but Stark did not feel so certain. While the two men talked, the sunset faded behind the mountains, and twilight darkened the still lake. The nondescript army built fires and opened their knapsacks, preparing to eat supper. Colonial troopers and rangers dressed in deerskins and homespun mingled freely with the scarlet-clad British Regulars.

How different a scene was taking place scarce twenty-four

hours later, where the French defenses turned back the British and colonials as Stark had feared they might!

"Masses of infuriated men who could not go forward and would not go back; straining for an enemy they could not reach and firing on an enemy they could not see; caught in the entanglement of fallen trees; ripped by briars; stumbling over logs; tearing through boughs; shouting, yelling, cursing, and pelted all the while with bullets that killed them by scores, stretched them on the ground or hung them on jagged branches in strange attitudes of death."

John Stark survived to taste the bitterness of defeat and mourn the loss of the gallant British peer who he always declared was the best commander for whom he ever fought. Before his fellows had recovered from the battle and withdrawn to plan their next move, he received word of his father's death and hurried to Derryfield. Old Archibald had gone to Portsmouth to settle a legal dispute and on his way home fallen deathly ill and died at Kingston. Here his younger son, Samuel, drove in a rude cart to bring the body back.

John stayed with his family only a short time, but long enough to marry Elizabeth "Molly" Page, daughter of Captain Caleb Page of Dunbarton, a slender girl, twenty years old, with brown hair and soft brown eyes. Those who knew her found signs of both strength and sweetness in her face. When scarcely more than a child she would sit by the pasture spring with a musket across her knees to keep the Indians from stealing her father's cattle.

The bridegroom did not tarry long on his honeymoon but rejoined the Rangers for the fall campaign, coming home again in the winter to help settle his father's affairs. The family was growing apace. Young Starks married into other pioneer families of the neighborhood, and children were born. He saw fighting in 1759 and was on his way to Quebec when he received news of its fall. This meant that all Canada would be ceded to Great Britain—hence the end of the war as the New Englanders saw it. Stark did not serve with the Rangers in 1760. He had too much to do at home, and he had developed a lasting dislike for the British, in spite of his admiration for Lord Howe. He felt that their polished and supercilious officers looked down on the Americans as a rout of ignorant and inferior peasants, fit only to perform heavy distasteful chores unsuited for gentlemen.

So he turned his back on the British army and all the issues of war, and went about the business of establishing himself as a substantial citizen of the Merrimack Valley. He had inherited land at Dunbarton besides some six hundred acres at Derryfield. In December, 1759, his first son, Caleb, was born at the home of Captain Page. The boy became a favorite with his grandfather and spent much of his early life there. John and Molly joined the widowed Eleanor at Derryfield to help her keep up the home place, and here their second son, Archibald, was born. With the encouragement of the town Stark built a sawmill at Dunbarton and kept it in operation as one of his many concerns. As his family grew he built himself a fine large house on a tract slightly to the north of his mother's, with two chimneys, many fireplaces, an ell, and sheds arranged about a sunny dooryard. He would allow neither paint nor paper in his home, preferring wainscot and paneling.

Busy about his personal affairs and growing family, he sought no public office during the next decade, but he kept aware of the drift of things: the Stamp Act and its repeal, the closing of Boston port and its occupation by British troops; the Boston Tea Party; the capture of the powder at Fort William and Mary. "Just what I would have expected," he may have thought, remembering his earlier distrust of the British. When meetings were called at Amherst, the county seat, to discuss raising troops for local protection, he attended them as the representative for the still tiny village of Derry-field. Perhaps he saw what was coming. Perhaps he suffered a grim surprise when news of the Battle of Lexington was brought to his sawmill one April day.

There are varying accounts as to exactly what John Stark did when he heard that his old partners in arms had spilled the blood of his countrymen at Lexington Green and Concord Bridge, but they all agreed that he rode off for Cambridge without delay, not stopping to recruit a company, but gathering up volunteers from the farms and villages as he went along. Some say that he walked out of the sawmill in his shirtsleeves, leaving the half-fitted boards to rot on their carriages till his return. According to some stories he carefully counted out three dollars and took it with him, leaving the rest of the family cash for Molly. By other accounts his haste was so great that he started off penniless and Molly ran after him with the forgotten wallet. At any rate, within twenty-four hours he had joined the troops at Medford and was soon chosen colonel by a show of hands at a tavern afterward known as New Hampshire Hall.

The New Hampshire assembly meeting at Exeter quibbled somewhat about his commission and summoned him to appear before them, which he did. Stark was blunt and abrupt in his manner, no politician to bargain tactfully. He said directly whatever he had to say, and he lacked the social polish, fine clothes, and elaborate graces of the leading citizens from the richer towns in the seacoast area. These men preferred their friends, Nathaniel Folsom and John Sullivan, who had little military experience and were to serve as undistinguished generals. But the rank and file of the New Hampshire volunteers wished to fight under John Stark and no other, and the assembly wisely confirmed him to the command of the First Regiment. The newly made colonel began at once to try to procure guns, ammunition, food, and medicine.

After long and ominous years, the threatened war had now come, and there was no turning backward. Paul Revere had left off silversmithing to go and print money for the new government. Adams and Hancock sat with the Congress in Philadelphia, debating ways and means to carry on. And on the tide marshes and village greens round Boston, John Stark found his place with those who would assemble and train the new army and lead it to its first test of strength at Bunker Hill.

A ring of American troops circled Boston, which still remained in possession of General Gage and the redcoats. During May the colonial officers decided to take and fortify the high ground above Charlestown village so that their guns could command the British fleet.

Scarcely had the red hot sun gone down on the evening of June 16 before the troops under Prescott and Putnam began to move out of their quarters toward Charlestown Neck. By midnight they had crossed Bunker Hill, the tall elevation at the head of the peninsula, and continued to Breed's Hill, lower down, nearer the water. Here they began to throw up earthworks and a redoubt. John Stark remained with his men at Winter Hill, striding between the campfires to see that all was in readiness should they be needed. Only that morning his fifteen-year-old son Caleb had arrived in camp with a musket on his shoulder. Caleb had slipped away from the Page home in Dunbarton on a horse given to him by his grandfather.

"Well, son, what are you here for?" demanded Stark.

"I can handle a musket and have come to try my fortune as a volunteer," replied Caleb stoutly.

"Very well," said the colonel, and turned to Captain George Reid. "Take him to your quarters. Tomorrow may be a busy day. After that we shall see what can be done for him."

And tomorrow proved indeed to be the busy day Stark had predicted.

When daylight came and the British saw the Americans still toiling doggedly at the new fortifications, they did not move at once, save to harass them with occasional shellfire from the fleet. Stark visited the scene, sent in a small detachment of his men when it was called for, and about midday crossed the Neck with the rest of his troops and led them to the grassy top of Bunker Hill.

A merciless June sun beat down on the gathering armies. Across the bay the bells of Boston were ringing and eager sightseers crowded the rooftops and steeples. Barges of British regiments, all scarlet, gold, and white, flanked by polished brass and gleaming cannon, swung out on the blue water and landed their cargoes at the point below the two hills. In Charlestown village on the right, most of the old gabled houses stood deserted in the midst of their gardens. Juniper bushes and tangled vines, bright daisies and buttercups, covered the peaceful pasture where blood would shortly flow.

To the left of the fortified hills a meadow ran down to a narrow beach along the shore of the Mystic River, and a rail fence crossed this meadow, providing the natural base for a bulwark some nine hundred feet long. After a brief conference with Putnam and Prescott, Stark moved his troops down to the rail fence and ordered them to bank it with new-cut hay, to extend it by heaping stones to the waterside. In a few minutes the New Hampshire men were at work.

Scarcely had they finished this hastily constructed shelter before the British attack began. Artillery fire covered the companies advancing on the right wing and the redoubt. Crack companies of Welsh Fusileers in their splendid uniforms drove toward the New Hampshire men in linsey-woolsey and hunting shirts, expecting little resistance. At the last moment John Stark stepped forth in front of his regiment and thrust a stake into the ground about eighty yards in front of the rail fence.

"There," he ordered, in the Scottish accent he had from his parents, "don't a man fire till the redcoats come up to that stake. If he does, I'll knock him down!"

At the end of the bloody fighting all the British dead lay between the stake and the fence, within the limits Stark had set, so well did his men obey him.

Three times the British charged the redoubt and the rail fence, and twice they were driven back. The New Hampshire sharpshooters inflicted great slaughter, but eventually Prescott's powder failed and he had to withdraw. Some of the overwhelmed and defeated Americans fled helter-skelter, but Stark's men moved over to cover the more orderly retreat. Once during the fighting a messenger reported to the colonel that his son Caleb had just been killed. Iron-souled John ordered the messenger back to his post, saying only that the enemy was in force in front and he had no time to talk of private affairs. Fortunately the report proved to be false.

With the twilight the British held Charlestown—they had burned the village during the afternoon—and the Americans had withdrawn to their camps in the surrounding hills. Both sides tended the wounded and tallied up the dead. British losses at the rail fence amounted to some 70 per cent of those who fought there, or some 465 men. Stark figured that he lost 16 of his men and 3 of Colonel Reed's. He said afterward that it seemed to him the British dead lay as thick as sheep in a fold.

General Howe, brother of Stark's old hero, had led the red-coats, and it was said that never afterward could he bear the sight of Americans entrenched upon a hill above him. General Gage shook his head and warned the home government that the rebels were aroused as no people had ever been and must forcibly be put down. "One more such victory," it was said in England, "and there will be nobody left alive to carry the good news home."

Except for occasional visits home, Stark remained with the troops around Boston until the British evacuated that city in March, 1776. After that he went on an unsuccessful mission to Canada under General Sullivan. Already he had begun to express resentment because neither his own state nor the Continental Congress seemed eager to give him the deserved promotion. After the costly defeat at Long Island, Washington's army retreated across New York and the Jersies and finally assembled at Coryell's Ferry on the Delaware to try to take measures to keep the British from overrunning Philadel-

phia. Here Stark joined them, and he is said to have counseled his chief, "Your men have relied too much on spades
and pickaxes [defense building]. If they are ever to establish
the independence of these states, it must be done with fire-
arms and courage."

"That is what we have agreed upon," replied Washington,
and unfolded the bold plan of a thrust at Trenton. In the
closing hours of a stormy Christmas Day, the Continental
Army crossed the ice-choked Delaware, sleet driving in their
faces, and marched by two separate routes toward the un-
suspecting town and its encampment of Hessians. Stark led
the right wing that approached by the River Road, and his
guns inflicted much slaughter. Half-asleep, scarce recovered
from their holiday revelry, the Germans fell like ripe fruit
into the hands of their attackers. As at Bunker Hill, the
bravery of their troops on this occasion put new life into the
cause of the colonists. Some have called it the turning point
of the Revolution. Skies brightened, from lonely New Hampshire backwoods to the plantations of the deep South. Perhaps this war for independence was not so hopeless after all.

Stark fought at Princeton, and when the army went into
winter quarters he left for New Hampshire to seek new re-
cruits. But he did not go until he had succeeded in getting
his men to reenlist, vowing that he himself would pay them
out of his own pocket if Congress continued to ignore their
claims.

But John Stark himself was the one most overlooked. In
February the Continental Congress appointed ten new brigadier generals, including Enoch Poore of New Hampshire,
and Stark's name did not appear on the list. To tell the truth,
the bluff, hard-driving country colonel was never popular

with "the Exeter crowd" who dominated the legislature, nor with the New Hampshire representatives in Congress. They distrusted Stark's independence, his "self-willedness" and "unbending character," and they overlooked his military skill and qualities of leadership.

This slight he protested to the assembly and declared that a man who would not stand for his office would not stand for his country. Commended, but still not promoted, he resigned and went back to his sawmill in Derryfield, saying that he wished to serve no longer with the Continental Army, but that if New Hampshire were attacked he would defend it.

Before the summer was over "the Exeter crowd" had called on him to do just that. By mid-July Burgoyne's advance down the Hudson seemed likely to spill over into the Grants—now Vermont. A British army advancing from that direction would set New Hampshire's battle line at the Connecticut River, something the province did not care to contemplate. They sent posthaste for John Stark, made him a brigadier general, and consented to his request, that he should be responsible to no other authority, meaning that he need not put himself under the generals of the army, most of whom he considered inferior in skill and experience, though he engaged in no open quarrels with anyone.

He proceeded at once to Fort Number Four on the Connecticut and began to assemble men and supplies. Volunteers rose in the middle of church services when they heard the call and poured forth to join him. New Hampshire had no trouble in assembling a regiment, but with supplies it was a different story. Stark had particular difficulty to get cooking kettles and rum. Eventually he led a thousand men to join with other colonists at Manchester, the rallying point. Here he entered into red-hot discussions with the Continental officers who assumed that Stark would put himself under their command. This he refused to do.

On August 13 while marching his men to a rendezvous not far from Bennington, Stark received word that a detachment of Burgoyne's forces was approaching, and he prepared to fight them. Burgoyne had sent out Lieutenant Colonel Baum with about five hundred men to try to capture some grain and flour supplies badly needed by his commissary. When Baum found his progress opposed, he climbed a wooded hill, entrenched himself, and sent for reinforcements.

Stark would have attacked them at once, except for a heavy rainstorm, but on the hot, bright afternoon of August 16, he put into operation his brilliant battle plan which operated like clockwork. Two attacking parties converged from opposite directions upon Baum, while Stark marched the remainder of his forces, including men from the Grants and from Massachusetts, to take the little bridge over the Walloomsac River and engage the Tories encamped on the neighboring bottomland. In an incredibly short time the fighting was over, and the British troops—mostly Hessians—had been killed, routed, or taken prisoner. The prisoners were tied two and two by long ropes and herded into Bennington. Stark found himself in possession of the field.

But just then reinforcements under Colonel Breyman came on, flanked by two cannon. From the woods, from the stone walls, from the alder bushes along the river, Stark's men loaded and fired, loaded and fired, cutting down this new attempt to project the Hudson campaign into New England. And by the fall of that misty summer twilight, the second battle of Bennington was over. Stark's men remained in possession of the field, bloody, tattered, exhausted, almost overwhelmed with the number of prisoners they had to feed, guard, and bivouac.

Many picturesque details of the campaign have survived. It was here, for instance, that Stark is supposed to have made his famous speech when pointing out to his men the direction of fire. "There are your enemies, boys, the Hessians and the Tories. We must beat them tonight, or Molly Stark sleeps a widow."

As they marched across a cornfield he gave the order for each man to thrust a sprig of corn husk through his hat. This would distinguish them from the local Tories who wore the same rough country garb. At the beginning of the first battle, while Stark waited for the two wings to close on Baum, he marched his forces round and round a circular hill, saying he did it to keep the Germans amused. During the melee some villain stole his favorite brown mare, and he later issued a bitter notice in the newspapers demanding her return.

Stark lay ill for a time after Bennington, and reported himself unfit for duty. Later he joined the army at Bemis Heights, willing to be put under the command of its leaders. His men, however, were not willing. They had engaged to fight only to defend New Hampshire. Feeling that New Hampshire was no longer threatened, when their terms of enlistment ran out they hastened home. Stark had to retire from the field because he could muster only three men. He went home, procured more troops, and played an active part at Saratoga by preventing reinforcements from joining Burgoyne from the north.

After the surrender he and his son Caleb went to General

Gates's headquarters and met the captured British officers. "Gentleman Johnny" Burgoyne took Stark to one side and talked to him about the old French war, how he hoped to write a history of it.

On October 5 John Hancock finally signed the commission which granted John Stark the rank of "Brigadier General in the Army of the United States, raised for the Defense of American liberty, and for the repelling of every hostile invasion thereof."

Stark spent the following winter in New Hampshire, busy at his sawmill and in the snowy woods, enjoying the company of his family and neighbors. A certain faction in Congress and the Army had begun an intrigue against Washington, which caused some confusion in military affairs. First an "irruption" into Canada was planned, which Stark was to lead, and he presented a campaign plan for it. Congress then decided to give the command to Lafayette and Conway. Notified that he was to serve under them, Stark replied in a businesslike fashion without rancor, asking how many men he should bring, when and where they meant to rendezvous. He received no answer.

Lafayette moved to Albany but attracted few men to the venture, and by spring his small force had melted away. Stark succeeded him there for a brief time. From Albany he wrote a letter of deep displeasure to his friends in the Grants when he heard of their design to take over some sixteen Connecticut River towns from New Hampshire. He asked also for a list of the New Hampshire men who had favored this treasonous objective.

Assigned to the Rhode Island campaign in its late, lethargic stages, he directed the occupation of Newport as the British abandoned it; he posted guards to maintain order and prevent looting. In October, 1780, Stark served as one of the judges who pronounced Major André guilty of espionage and condemned him to death. He led various forays around Westchester and Staten Island, and on November 30 asked to retire because of ill health and financial impoverishment. He requested that Washington send him what amounted to fifty dollars hard cash to pay for his trip home. Washington released him from duty, but replied ruefully that the military chest was empty and he had no money for his own needs.

Stark somehow managed to get to Derryfield, but in the summer of 1781 he went back to Albany to take command of the northern forces. The main currents of the war had moved southward now, but danger always threatened from Canada, increased by the traitorous dealings of men in the Grants. Shortly afterward, however, came the surrender of Cornwallis and the virtual end of the war. John Stark returned home for the last time, companioned across the winter countryside by the faithful Caleb. Here he passes out of our national history.

But the seasoned old campaigner had a new child in the cradle and forty years still ahead of him. Troubled by rheumatism and ill health, he was rarely so incapacitated that he could not go on being a forceful citizen and businessman in his native Merrimack Valley. He did not engage in politics, but he made his views known on almost every problem, political or economic, that beset the growing country.

He refused to install a pump and system of wooden pipes at his mill pond, because, he said, he had "no desire to make a slave of water."

He preferred states rights to central government—though

loyal to the new Constitution—favored Jefferson's political philosophy and "Mr. Madison's War."

He never "took much stock" in plans to build a canal and a bridge over the Merrimack, but he lived to see both carried out.

He favored inoculation against smallpox when many folk of his time still feared and distrusted it.

He finally received the rank of major general with a grim triumph at the delayed honor.

Molly Stark never slept a widow, but died well before her husband in 1814. The aging man called out mournfully as her body was borne from the house, "Good-bye, Molly, we sup no more together on this earth." Though he lived on, cared for by his numerous family, until May 8, 1822, perhaps he took his last bull by ye horns when he wrote explaining why he could not attend the Bennington anniversary celebration in 1809.

> I received yours of the 23rd instant, containing your fervid expressions of friendship and your very polite invitation to meet with you to celebrate the 16th of August in Bennington. As you observe, "I can never forget that I commanded American troops on that day." . . . they were men who had not learned the art of submission, nor had they been trained to the art of war. But our "astonishing success" taught the enemies of liberty that undisciplined freemen are superior to veteran slaves. Nothing could afford me greater pleasure than to meet your "Brave Sons of Liberty" on the fortunate spot. But as you justly anticipate, the infirmities of old age will not permit, for I am now fourscore and one years old, and the lamp of life is almost spent. . . .
>
> In case of my not being able to attend, you wish my sentiments. These you shall have, as free as the air we breathe.

As I was then, as I am now, the friend of the equal rights of men, of representative democracy, of republicanism, and the Declaration of Independence, the great charter of our national rights, and of course a friend to the indissoluble union, and the constitution of the United States. . . .

I shall remember, gentlemen, the respect you and the inhabitants of Bennington and its neighborhood have shown me, until I go to the country from which no traveler returns. I must soon receive my marching orders.

With it he sent also the toast, "Live free or die; death is not the worst of evils," part of which became the official motto of his state, New Hampshire.

Patriot, frontiersman, general, John Stark has still another significance in American history. If students in later times wonder just what a "rugged individualist" was like, they may study John Stark and learn.

Chapter 10

———◆◆◇◆◆———

SAMUEL MOREY

It is doubtful if Samuel Morey, inventor and pioneer in
American mechanics, remembered in later years his first sight
of the Connecticut River. But he was to be, for most of his
eighty productive years, a Connecticut River man, and his
genius might have directed itself in a different course if the
dark, full-flowing waters of New England's heart stream had
not been a part of his everyday living.

Samuel was born in Hebron, Connecticut, on October 23,
1762, the son of Israel and Martha Palmer Morey. But a little
less than four years later, in January, 1766, Israel loaded his
wife and three tiny children into an oxcart and started the
two-hundred-mile journey to Orford, New Hampshire, the
pioneer community where he had chosen to build a new
home. Only a family or two had preceded them up the winding valley of the Connecticut. The road did not extend beyond Charlestown village, old Fort Number Four. Perhaps
that was why Israel chose to make the journey when the
ground was frozen and travel easier than in muddy spring or
during the intolerable heat of July. He himself commented
later that "the trip was accomplished without accident or

incident." The Mann family, also from Hebron, had come to Orford ahead of him, and they sheltered the Moreys and helped them to build a cabin and, in the next summer, to plant and harvest a crop.

For the next few years the town and the Morey children along with it went through their growing time. Israel, a man of great physical strength and mental vigor, took an active part in town affairs. He helped to lay out the roads and the town mall, established three mills, and ran a tavern and a blacksmith shop. He served as town clerk, was an ardent Son of Liberty just before the outbreak of the Revolution, and rose to the rank of general in that war.

In 1770 church services had to be held in an unfinished barn, but by 1773 the town could boast of a church and school, over four hundred acres of cleared land, and some two hundred and twenty-eight residents. The crude stump fences and log cabins were giving place to rows of thriving shade trees and neat frame houses along the common and Bridge Street running down to the ferry. Orford from its early days was a planned and beautiful town, and Israel Morey helped to plan it.

The Moreys were a reading family and sent to Hartford and New Haven for books, since the Orford Social Library was not established till 1797. When the books arrived, young Samuel turned impatiently away from histories and sermons, but read with great eagerness those volumes devoted to natural history and science. During his school days he began to make small gadgets useful about the farm and in his mother's kitchen. While still in his teens he built with his own hands a little workshop where he could perform experiments and repair broken tools and implements the neighbors brought to him. According to legend they used to call him "Mr. Fixit," for after he had mended an object he would run his hand carefully over its surface to test the smoothness of his work and murmur, "Now I have fixed it, and it is better than it was before." Practical always, and full of common sense, he did not aim for theoretical knowledge, but only "to get up a machine that will do the work better, quicker, and easier than could be done by hand."

The 1780's were troubled years for the Moreys. Israel had supported the attempts of sixteen New Hampshire river towns, including Orford, to join Ethan Allen's free and independent republic of Vermont. Angered when this movement failed, he crossed the river to Fairlee, built a house, and established a lumber business. For the rest of his life he maintained active interests in both towns, and he did not stay angry long. Those who remembered him in his old age described him as placid, easy, and benign, riding his gentle horse at a slow trot up Bridge Street and along the mall, a hat like a Quaker's set on his white hair, and a cloak flung over his arm in case the fickle valley weather should change.

Samuel, now a grown man, divided his time between the family business and his experiments. He had become deeply interested in the possibilities of steam, more interested in making use of it to move boats up and down the river highroad flowing past his front door.

He was not by any means the first American to come up with such an idea. William Henry had built a steam-driven boat in 1763 and tested it on Conestoga Creek at Lancaster, Pennsylvania, but it proved unsuccessful. William Rumsey of Virginia produced such a boat and demonstrated it on the Potomac in 1784, but could not obtain a patent. John Fitch of Philadelphia designed a different model in 1785 and built a better one in 1789 that served as a passenger boat on the Delaware and was said to be able to travel at a speed of seven miles an hour. If Samuel heard of these other boats, he knew nothing of the details of their construction. He went on working at his own, and in 1792 he finally succeeded in fitting a steam boiler to a small boat and making it move across the waters of Fairlee Pond.

For the next two years he worked hard to perfect his steamboat, but he could not devote all his time to it. He had been chosen as consulting engineer for a system of locks and canals to be built along the river making it navigable from Windsor Locks in Connecticut to Olcott's Falls not far from Hanover. English engineers came over to do the job, but they needed the advice of a local expert familiar with the river and both its banks, with the ledges of stubborn rock they would have to cut through. The project took years to complete, and Samuel helped to solve its worst problems. He was put in charge of the mechanical operation of the locks once they were installed.

In 1792 he launched his boat for an experimental trip on the Connecticut to see how well it would perform against the current of this powerful stream. With only one friend as a witness he chose to make the attempt on a Sunday morning while all the townspeople were attending church services and could not line the banks to watch him, shout directions, and jeer if he should fail. But he did not fail. Later, the friend, John Mann, Jr., first white male child born in Orford, son of the pioneer family who had helped the Moreys on their coming, described the amazing sight.

Samuel crouched in the tiny boat hardly big enough to

hold himself, a steam boiler, and a handful of wood to keep the fire going. He shoved off into the slow, full current. The craft faltered, spun a little, and then began to breast the stream, boiler puffing, paddlewheel dripping. It moved steadily upriver toward Fairlee. Its maker had tried it out secretly in quiet coves, but never against the full strength of the river before. Now he piled more wood on the fire and waited, still cautious. But he kept forging ahead. The banks began to slip by him. Then he straightened up and waved exultantly to Johnny Mann. Scows, canoes, dugouts, even sailboats, could pass into history now. Samuel Morey had found a way to run a boat by steam.

Now he was ready for all the world to see his invention, and the spectacle of the little boat puffing and splashing along the river became familiar to the people of Orford and Fairlee. Quick-witted and friendly, always eager to help his neighbors, Sam was popular, and both towns rejoiced at his success. His genius did not make him a recluse or a hermit. He remained in the center of life, active in civic affairs and business.

Now he wanted to try his boat on salt water, so he took it downriver, all the way to Long Island Sound and thence to New York. He had a larger model now that could carry passengers and maintain a speed of nearly six miles an hour. On one demonstration trip between New York and Greenwich several important guests came aboard and made the acquaintance of the inventor. One of these was Robert R. Livingston, member of a wealthy New York family, Chancellor of the State of New York.

The real truth of the dealings between Livingston and Samuel Morey is lost in the fog of history. No complete, detailed, and honest biography of Morey has ever been written. Livingston's biographers ignore the Connecticut River man. No scholar has yet made it his business to explore their relationship. This much is certain: Livingston did examine Morey's boat and talked with the inventor.

The tradition among friends and supporters of Morey's claim to having invented the first steamboat runs something like this. Livingston is said to have been deeply interested in Morey's boat, but suggested improvements in its structure. Morey had placed his engine in the bow, and Livingston thought it would work better if placed in the center or on the side. Once Samuel was back in Orford continuing with his experiments the two corresponded. According to one account Livingston was so much interested that he actually made the long journey to carry on negotiations with the inventor in his own workshop.

A Dr. Allison, of Bordentown, New Jersey, entered the picture briefly in 1797. He headed a group of men who were eager to establish a steamboat line between Bordentown and Philadelphia. Samuel went to Bordentown and built a boat than ran successfully and fulfilled their requirements. But the group ran out of money, and he went home to Orford to perfect his invention further.

In 1798 John Fitch died in New York, heart-broken and in poverty because his steamboat had failed. Livingston promptly acquired the monopoly Fitch had owned, which gave him the exclusive rights to steam navigation on the rivers of New York State for the next twenty years, provided that within a year he could produce a boat that would travel at the rate of four miles an hour. Livingston did build a boat, but it failed to meet the test. In 1801 he went as United States minister to France, and in France he met Robert Fulton. Fulton, an American artist and inventor, had been living abroad for some years and had devised a new type of canal lock and a kind of underwater torpedo. He, too, was interested in building ships that would run by steam. Fulton and Livingston became fast friends, and Livingston passed on his working knowledge of Morey's invention.

This is only one version of the story, but according to it, after Livingston returned to New York, Morey made many trips there to see him. Some say Fulton and Morey met face to face and had dealings and conferences. Other tellers of the tale insist that they never met, that all Fulton knew of Samuel's work was what he had learned through Livingston. One persistent legend has it that Samuel Morey turned over all his drawings, patterns, and models to the Livingston-Fulton interests; that they promised him $100,000 in cash if he would go home and make a few changes.

But when he returned to New York, the changes made, there had been also changes in the projected business arrangements, changes, too, in the climate of the friendship, for he no longer received a warm welcome. Now, it seemed, he would be allotted shares in a theoretical stock company but not a penny in cash. Samuel was stunned and insisted that the original agreement be honored. They tried to bargain with him, offered to call the experimental ship "The Lady Morey," and added a small cash settlement. Samuel proudly refused. He went home empty-handed and, having no redress, insisting that his invention had been stolen.

The Morey model which Fulton and Livingston had knowledge of has been described this way:

It was a rotary engine balanced on a disk 1 and $\frac{1}{8}$ inches in diameter, the disk attached to a rod connecting with the boiler. In this disk are two openings, $\frac{1}{2}$ by $\frac{1}{8}$ inches; one connected with the boiler as mentioned above, the other opening into the air. This forms the valve seat. The valves consist of a second disk, with corresponding openings, fitting exactly upon the surface of the first disk, and from the two openings in this upper disk are tubes leading to the extremities of the cylinder. The piston rod is attached to a stationary crank in the center of the machine, and the outward and inward movements of the piston cause the revolution of the upper disk, cylinder, etc., upon the lower disk; thus bringing the valves or openings in the upper disk, alternately over the steam tube and the escape opening of the lower disk.

The entire length of the machine is 6 and $\frac{1}{2}$ inches. The cylinder, which is of brass, is 1 and 15/16 inches in length and 1 and $\frac{1}{2}$ inches in diameter. Length of stroke is 1 and 3/16 inches. The piston, which is of cast iron, is 1 and $\frac{3}{8}$ inches in diameter, with a groove on the edge, in which twine is used for packing. The piston rod plays on friction rollers.

Some time later, in August, 1807, Robert Fulton ran his *Clermont*—named after the Livingston country place—up the river from New York to Albany, and ever since has been credited with having invented the first steamboat. Morey always felt that the *Clermont* was constructed after his own model that had been pirated by Fulton. Most historians have continued to prefer Fulton's claims, but Morey, too, has his defenders. The subject deserves the attention of some openminded scholar.

If Sam's only achievement had been his steamboat, his story might be ended here; but far from that, it was but one of his many experiments and inventions—not even the most important.

In 1793 he invented a spit that would turn by steam. No meat ever tasted more delicious than that roasted evenly on a revolving iron rod in the fireplace. But the spit must be turned by hand or by one of the pitiful little "turnspit dogs," hairless, frequently scorched beasts, who were harnessed and driven round to keep the roast in motion. Certainly the animal world owed a debt to Sam Morey for making this custom no longer necessary.

Always fond of animals himself, he was, nevertheless, an ardent hunter, and would range the woods around the base of Cube Mountain for wolves, bears, and catamounts, shooting them on the run. Said to be the best shot in Orford or Fairlee either, he kept three fine guns always in the pink of condition. But he would never shoot the sleek, tall-antlered deer. Instead he maintained an enclosed park for a number of the species whom he had domesticated and made pets of. He studied them and wrote little essays about their habits and personalities.

The turnspit patent was one of the first fifty patents issued by the United States Patent Office and bore the signatures of Washington and Jefferson. Other patents followed quickly: a steamboat patent in 1795, and the next year a patent for the method and machinery by which water could be raised by wind power; in 1799 another water engine and improvements for it.

By this time Samuel was married to Hannah Avery and had built himself a fine mansion on the Ridge rising just above Orford and facing the river. This high terrace was an old river level from which the waters had receded thousands of years before Samuel Morey's time. He built a house of the Bulfinch type which remains today, white and gracefully planned, a beautiful example of late eighteenth-century architecture. Years later he built a home next to it for his daughter Almira when she married, and other mansions quite as lovely sprang up nearby.

We do not know much about wife Hannah, but we do have a letter she wrote to Samuel from Orford in April, 1793, when the new house was a-building. He was away on one of his frequent trips to demonstrate his inventions, but these lines must surely have turned his heart if not his footsteps homeward.

"Work progresses slowly," she wrote, "because of frost in the ground which prevents digging the cellar. The workmen are much hampered for lumber, especially boards. Ground is much covered with snow. Not a ton of hay in Orford, and it is pitiful to hear the poor cattle crying for something to eat." No complaint for her own loneliness and discomfort, only for the misery of the animals. It is our guess that Hannah made Samuel a good helpmate.

"Captain Sam," as he was affectionately called, completed his house on the Ridge in 1799, the year of Washington's death. A new America was growing up in which courtly colonial gentlemen felt themselves to be out of place and sighed for the good old days. John Adams would shortly retire to his Quincy acres to rusticate through a prolonged and somewhat bewildered old age. Ethan Allen and John Hancock had burned themselves out and died before they felt too much pressure to adjust to the changing scene, to the growing importance of machines and industrialism, to the fact that while the frontier still existed it was not in New

England any more. Of all the Revolutionary generation perhaps Paul Revere with his practical mind and inventive
genius fitted best into the nineteenth century. The develop-
ing economy stood in desperate need of creative craftsmen,
and Paul took full advantage of a tide that set in his favor.
Samuel Morey, a generation younger, not only fitted into our
fast-emerging modern world, but he was a part of it. He felt
at home in it. He helped to bring it about.

For the next thirty-five years he lived in his spacious mansion, constantly experimenting and taking out new patents.
Land poor, sometimes, he remained for the most part prosperous because he never neglected the family business interests, chiefly lumber. Starving in a garret was not for Sam. He
just would not have seen any sense in it. He maintained all
his life that Fulton and Livingston had stolen his first important invention, his steamboat, and he felt bitter, but he
did not sulk and brood. He had been cheated in a business
deal, but it would not happen again, not if he could help it.
He did not consider his inventions works of art for which
honor would be sufficient pay. Neither did he care to amass
a huge fortune. He produced them, patented them, and sold
the patents for honest prices when it was to his practical advantage, for he did not care to manufacture them in quanti-
ties. He was chiefly interested in creating devices that would
perform the tasks of everyday living more efficiently, and he
wanted to see these devices in general use.

Before we go on to describe some of Sam's inventions, let
us try to take a closer look at him as his neighbors saw him,
swinging up Bridge Street, bending over his work bench,
strolling with his friends at evening under the tall elms on
Orford's mall. One early writer describes him as "a size larger

than Daniel Webster, with a frown that would stop any man, but his broad sympathetic smile always created a world of peace and confidence." He could never have been a successful gambler, for far from having a poker face, one could always tell by looking at his expression just what he thought and felt about any matter being discussed. Nor is it likely he would have taken to dice and cards, feeling as he did about drunkenness, their frequent companion.

Once when he was a boy a church deacon came to his father's tavern and called for a glass of rum. After being served he began to talk about the drought and how he doubted if any of the local farmers would raise much of a crop that season. Then he took another glass and said he hoped the town would see a revival of religion. His third glass produced a stronger if somewhat muddled sentiment. He averred then, loudly and with much thumping on the bar, that he hoped there would not be another drop of rain till they had one of the greatest revivals ever known, if the crops went into the ground and all the people died. That settled the question for Sam, he told a nephew years later. "Rum and religion had better be kept separate."

Another anecdote concerns his attitude toward the young fry, one that would do credit to a modern child psychologist. As an old man later described it:

When there was to be a man hanged in Haverhill, ten miles from here (I was a lad then), he did not wish the boys to go to see the execution. He told us if we would stay at home and have a game of ball, he would give to all such a good supper and plenty of lemonade. He joined with us, greatly to our delight and enjoyment, and seemingly to his own. To us it was a great day. We found it, as he had told us, "better than a hang-ing."

Though he represented his town several times in the state legislature, he never sought office nor wished for a political career. When any election loomed and his name was men-tioned as a candidate, he would take some of his friends out into the woods, ostensibly to go hunting. Once in the privacy of the thick-growing evergreens that clothed the hills round Orford, he would ask his companions if they did not know of some good man who should be chosen instead of himself, for he never wished to stand in the way of a better man.

Always charitable, he supported several poor families, and would frequently go to the tax collector offering to pay the taxes of any of the deserving poor. Being farsighted, too, he would lay in supplies of hay and grain against the times when the crops failed and famine threatened. Then he would sell to the destitute at a fair price, but if speculators came and sought to buy from him in order to resell at extortionate profits, he would threaten to set his dogs on them.

For the first three decades of the nineteenth century Sam kept the Patent Office busy. Many of these patents were for refinements on his original use of steam. In 1812 he registered a device to make use of hot air as a source of power. In 1813 he reported on a series of experiments in air-conditioning, retension and redistribution of heat, and the conveyance up-chimney of smoke and noxious gases. In this year, too, he received a patent for heating a group of rooms from one fire-place. Orford is far to the north, and New Hampshire winters are cold. It is easy to understand why the owner of a large and spacious house should have been concerned with finding better methods for heating it. Perhaps Hannah shivered in her paneled parlor and urged that he get on with the idea.

He was granted patents, too, for tide and water wheels, and produced a carburretted hydrogen gas which could be lighted to give off a glow of one hundred candle power. In 1814 he patented a revolving steam engine which he later sold for $5000—his top price—to John Sullivan of Boston. Sullivan built a number of successful boats by this design, one of which went to South Carolina and proved to be ideal for towing heavy loads against the strong currents of the Santee and Congaree rivers.

In the following year he patented "The American Water Burner" and "The Treble Pipe Steamboiler" and carried on all sorts of experiments with combustible gases, also with carbonated waters. The limestone hills of his native town provided excellent material for the latter type of investigation. Sam was always a man for making use of what lay close to hand. And he did not try to patent or market these results, but gave them away to those who could use them.

Finally, in the spring of 1826 he achieved his greatest triumph when a new patent grant arrived for him at the tiny post office in Orford. This patent was for his vapor engine, forerunner of the internal combustion engine which would make self-propelled vehicles possible, and with them our world of today.

It is now difficult to imagine what our lives would be like without the internal combustion engine. The automobile is only one aspect of what this invention meant, one aspect of the life we know, but how much of that life depends upon the automobile. Without it there would be no commuters, no Sunday drivers, cross-country tours, or week-end vacation trips; no ambulances, buses, delivery vans, or racing cars. Men would be forced to live close to their jobs, hence no suburbs. Every family would have to keep a horse or be unable to travel more than a few miles from home. Think how the pace of life would slow, distances increase, and cities draw further apart and into themselves, how our habits would change, even the landscape itself. And think of Samuel Morey, who knew a world like this and changed it all.

Did he know what he was doing when he toiled away in his workshop at the edge of the quaint little village green with his deer grazing just beyond the window? Did he realize the implications of the models that grew under his patient fingers, implications suited to the needs of a busy, rich, expanding, productive nation, rather than to a world of quaint villages and deer?

There is some evidence that he did, at least that he felt the canal system had no future before it, that it would be replaced by steam-driven vehicles. Charles Duryea, "father of the American automobile," who developed the first gas engine in 1892 and organized the first commercial automobile company shortly afterward, always gave credit to Samuel Morey for the initial work. He insisted that Morey's vapor engine was the forerunner of the gas engine, that "Morey's idea further developed made possible the automobile and the airplane."

Though it was not perfected until later, Morey's vapor engine received much attention when news of it first appeared. It was written up in important journals such as Silliman's *Journal of American Science,* to which Morey himself made contributions, Professor Silliman always having been an admirer of his. The inventor himself called this his "Turpentine Engine," for he found that turpentine vapor mixed with air produced the best explosive power for it, and he wrote, "It remains for me to have the engine applied in a carriage on a railroad, and when this is done I should think I have done my part." Plans for national demonstrations, promotion, and production were talked of, but nothing came of it just then. The internal combustion engine had appeared before America was ready for it.

Samuel Morey's later life would have been an overwhelming tragedy for a weaker man, less used to standing up under misfortune. His wife Hannah died in 1822. In 1830 he lost both his only grandchild and his only child, Almira. She was the wife of Judge Leonard Wilcox, one of Orford's most learned and respected men. With them perished Morey's own line, his flesh and blood link with the future. No heirs remained to carry on his genius and his name.

In 1835 the old inventor moved across the river to Fairlee and built himself a cottage near Fairlee Pond, now Lake Morey. He called the cottage Bonny Vale and continued his experiments there. He dug a canal and worked out a miniature system of locks and dams, studied the habits of fish, and lived out his days in serene prosperity. When he died on April 17, 1843, he left a comfortable estate besides his two homes: four horses, a houseboat on the lake, a treadmill with side paddlewheels, a modern and efficient sawmill, and thirty-four hundred acres of virgin timber. Characteristically he left no debts, and he still remains a source of great local pride around Orford and Fairlee.

For years the legend persisted that one of his boats was

sunk by his "enemies" and lay at the bottom of Lake Morey under a dense growth of pickerel grass. Some said this was the boat Fulton knew; others that it was a pleasure boat, painted red and white, called the *Aunt Sally*. The New Hampshire Antiquarian Society made a search for this sunken treasure, hoping to discover one of Morey's early experimental models still in existence, but were unable to find it. Dr. Hosford, Morey's physician, reported that the Fulton boat had been "worked up into firewood." Morey himself never mentioned a sunken boat, and no one was ever known who would be likely to take such action against him.

Most authorities are willing to grant Samuel Morey the honor of first discovering the principle of the internal combustion engine. And this is surely enough to win him a place among America's foremost inventors. Perhaps he has no need to claim, too, the invention of the first steamboat. But to the end of his days he stubbornly affirmed that Fulton and Livingston had done him wrong.

Chapter 11

————◦◦◦————

ELI WHITNEY

When President Ezra Stiles of Yale College looked out across New Haven green on April 30, 1789, he saw a different sight from the one that Jonathan Edwards had seen when he came to town some seventy years before. Today's tall elms did not yet beautify it, and the old gravestones of colonial times had not been removed. But the college now occupied five buildings on the west side of the green, including stern-faced Connecticut Hall, the president's house and chapel, a library of sorts, and a museum. A board fence ran around it painted red and white. It was an establishment that drew young men from every state in the new federal union, and Mr. Stiles was proud to be at the head of it. Now he turned away from the pleasing view and wrote in his diary.

> "I gave a philosophy lecture. Examined and admitted a freshman of Yale College. G. Washington inaugurated and proclaimed at New York."

Perhaps he thought of the splendid ceremonial procession winding through the crooked old streets of lower Manhattan and wished that he might be there. Perhaps he thought in-

stead of the freshman who had stood before him that afternoon, a large, heavy young man with a hooked nose, black
hair, and keen, deepset black eyes, who had signed the reg-
ister, "Eli Whitney."

Born in Westborough, Massachusetts, on December 8,
1765, to Eli Whitney and his wife, Elizabeth Fay Whitney,
young Eli, the future inventor, spent a boyhood not unlike
that of other lads of his time growing up in a frugal, thrifty
New England farm family. In the freezing winters he carried
water and forked down hay for sixty head of cattle. During
the other three seasons he worked in the fields, seeding, hoe-
ing, and harvesting. And every day he spent as many hours as
possible in his father's workshop, learning to use hand tools
and the lathe, repairing household articles, and adding small
improvements of his own.

News of the battles of Lexington, Bunker Hill, Long Island, Trenton, and finally Yorktown, traveled across the long
sandy valleys of inland Massachusetts without touching the
Whitney family too closely. The older Eli, while in sympathy
with the patriot cause, had many responsibilities to keep him
from taking up a musket. He held several town offices and
served as justice of the peace, and in 1779 his ailing wife died
and left him with four young children. Later he brought
home a stepmother for his children, but she had daughters of
her own whom she favored, and the young Eli began very
early to give his brothers and sister the protective love and
care that lasted throughout his lifetime.

A mild, affable boy, said at the age of twelve to have had
more general knowledge than most grown men in the county,
he spent more and more of his time in the workshop. He
could take a watch apart and put it together again. He con-

structed a fiddle that made "tolerable good music." The war brought about a scarcity of many imported goods such as nails, and Eli coaxed his father to let him set up a forge and produce nails to sell to the countryside.

Succeeding in this, he took a three-day trip, visiting the workshops of other ingenious Yankees to add to his own "know-how." On the journey he hired a man to assist him and increase his output, showing himself to be a business man as well as an inventive craftsman. When English nails became available again at the end of the war, Eli merely shifted his product and began to manufacture walking sticks and hat pins to hold women's bonnets in place.

Having learned all that the little Westborough school could teach him, he turned his attention to the farm and the workshop and expressed no wish for further education until the fall of 1783. Then at the age when many young men had completed college Eli first mentioned to his father that he would like more schooling. Dollars were hard to come by in the Whitney family, and his stepmother vehemently opposed this extravagance. The countryside had not yet begun to recover from the long war and inflation made prices unbearably high, even for rich folk. The way would not be easy for any grown man seeking to go back and be a schoolboy again. But Eli knew what he wanted, and he set about getting it.

First he secured a position as a school teacher in Grafton for seven dollars a month and his living. For several years he kept village schools in winter and studied at Leicester Academy during summer term. He had the Bible, the *New England Primer,* and Noah Webster's *Spelling Book* to help him, but no arithmetic texts existed. He had to keep the fire going and discipline the scholars, but it would seem from his own comments about his work that he took it to heart and tried to make a good job of it. Practical always, he made a model of a quill pen and showed his scholars how to make duplicates for their own use. In his spare moments he busied his thoughts with the problem of perpetual motion.

In 1788 he was pronounced "a person of good Sober life and conversation, and well qualified to keep a Grammar school—having acquired a good acquaintance with the Latin and Greek languages and also the English Grammar—at Leicester Academy." An illness threatened his life that summer, but by March, 1789, quiet, long-time perseverance won. His father drove him to Brookfield where he could take the coach for New Haven, shook his hand, put money in it, and wished him well.

Eli had perhaps chosen Yale in preference to Harvard because his own teachers had been Yale men, but he did not feel ready yet to go directly to the college and present himself for examination. Instead he lodged for a month with Reverend Elizur Goodrich of Durham, a friend of President Stiles. Mr. Goodrich coached him in mathematics and he formed a lasting friendship with Elizur, Jr. A few weeks later he was admitted to the college in mid term. His intelligence and maturity making up for his lack of interest in philosophy and literature.

New Haven, a worldly, sophisticated city with a certain stateliness and order, must have awakened deep excitement and satisfaction in the Westborough farm youth who had striven so hard to go beyond Westborough. Ships from all over the world put in there, and the taverns echoed with the gossip not only of Boston and New York, but of Philadelphia, Charleston, London. Young men from the Hudson Valley and the Pennsylvania frontier shared the college facilities with ingenious, reserved Yankees and dashing plantation heirs from the South. Perhaps we may dare to picture Eli sitting with some young southerner, their books neglected and the candles burning low, listening to the other man's description of broad acres in need of a new crop to replace tobacco and indigo.

Colleges continued to train young men chiefly for the ministry, but they also prepared them for teaching and the bar. The course of study was not what it had been in the days of Cotton Mather, and although it was still dominated by the dead languages and divinity, new elements closer to human living had crept in. The library held less than three thousand books, most of them old and of little interest to Eli—but it did contain Newton's *Principia*. And the museum boasted a wide display of scientific instruments: an air pump and electrical machine, a quadrant, levers, pulleys, toothed wheels, wedges and screws, and a micrometer.

Eli doubtless enjoyed the natural philosophy lectures best, but he shrewdly realized that he had come to Yale for more than information and academic knowledge. He had come to learn the social graces, how to speak and orate, wear the right clothes and use the right tableware and conduct himself easily in public. Always handsome, his affable and friendly ways and his quick intelligence made him popular. He had no troubles except lack of money. His father sent him what he could, and Eli himself worked at coloring maps and performing chores for richer students. He completed his course not too much in debt, and marched in the gala commencement procession in September, 1792, while fireworks trailed their comets and blazing serpents above the college yard. Disappointed in a teaching post he had expected to receive in New York, he agreed on President Stiles' recommendation to make the journey to South Carolina to tutor the children of a Major Dupont. Here, he thought, at an excellent salary he could save money and read law. He felt apprehensive about the effect an unfamiliar climate might have on his health, and he set out a little drearily for Manhattan where he would meet his traveling companions, one Phineas Miller of Connecticut and a Mrs. Greene.

Eli's gloom and apprehension proved justified. He was seasick all the way down the sound, and when the packet ran ashore on the rocks of Hell Gate, he and several other passengers hired a wagon to take them into the city. Here he suffered immediate exposure to smallpox and had to undergo inoculation. Recovered from this he embarked for Savannah which he reached after six days of distressing seasickness. But his instant liking and admiration for his new friends made it all worthwhile. Catherine Greene, widow of General Nathanael Greene, now approaching forty, had lost none of the grace, spirit, and charm, none of the delightful femininity that had made her almost as famous as her husband. Whether it was a ballroom at Newport, a smoky hut in the freezing winter at Valley Forge, or the banquet table of a lush plantation, Catherine's warm smile, her dauntless courage, and her eternal fascination made her welcome everywhere. She saw at once the true worth of the practical young New Englander and gave him her wholehearted friendship.

Nor was Phineas Miller far behind her in this. Phineas, a Yale graduate, had gone south to Greene's plantation, Mulberry Grove, in the last year of the General's life to tutor the Greene children. Afterwards he had stayed on to help the widow manage the estate and become as one of the family. Loyal, able, affectionate, and cultivated, he was to reassure Eli many times when the troubled inventor lost faith in himself.

They landed at Savannah where Eli found the houses to be weathered, mean, and below his expectations. The fields had but lately been harvested of crops alien to New England. After a week's visit at Mulberry Grove, he planned to cross the river into South Carolina and seek out Major Dupont, but he never reached the Major's. Was it Catherine's charm that held him while the winter slipped away, or the gracious, southern ways of life so different from those of the bleak Massachusetts countryside? Or was it the ebb and flow of his own mind as he worked by trial and error at the growing model in the basement room that detained him? Probably it was a mixture of all three, but the last one most of all.

Mulberry Grove, where Eli Whitney's famous cotton gin— "gin" a short form of "engine"—was first constructed, occupied some two thousand acres of the richest rice lands in Georgia. Its elegant mansion stood in the midst of moss-covered oaks, a stately Georgian house with a great brick chimney at either end and a fan-lighted front door. Behind it stood the stables, the coach house, and the poultry house. A detached kitchen seemed strangest of all to the New Englander, who was used to thinking of the kitchen as the heart of the house—perhaps the only room warm enough to live in when winter came. And around it lay vast rice fields and corn fields, beyond the orchard and garden. Each season brought its special table delicacies; green peas and lettuce, peaches, pears, figs, nectarines, apricots, strawberries, and melon. Catherine's servants understood pickling and preserving, spices, and sauces and seasoning; preparing huge roasts and hot breads and fabulous desserts. Nor did good wine ever lack. This profusion must have seemed almost wicked to Eli, used to stewed pumpkin and salt pork and rum. But if he had such thoughts he kept them to himself.

There were always guests thronging to the ample board, and as he talked with Catherine's neighbors he was quickly made aware of what they considered the South's greatest problem. That he would be the one to solve it, he did not know then.

Nor was this only a southern problem. America was a new nation. Although free of former restrictions, it no longer enjoyed the support and protection of the mother country. If it was to advance itself and become one of the great trading nations of the world, it must produce exports, either in manufactures or raw materials, that other countries could use in manufacture. Whitney's own New England had little to offer but fish, rum, and decreasing supplies of lumber. Only the East Indian and China traders now prospered there. The skilled artisans in the middle colonies found their operations hampered by the poverty following the war. In the South the rice fields had fallen off, indigo was no longer in demand, while tobacco was in oversupply and many of its plantations worn out. America needed a new product to sell to the great markets abroad.

In England the industrial revolution had come about and advanced till the constantly improved machines in the cloth mills whirred frantically, producing more and more yards of cloth. But sometimes they fell silent, workers went hungry, and woven fabrics were in short supply. Cotton from the West Indies, cotton from Brazil, from Smyrna, from India, from Egypt could not fill the demand. Potentially America should produce huge supplies of cotton. They had unlimited acreage there, and in many sections the climate was favorable. What was the matter with American cotton? Eli did not know, but he found out, as the planters sat over their pipes and wine in the late autumn twilights at Mulberry Grove.

Southern cotton, he learned, was of two kinds. In the sea islands grew the long, silky-fibred kind, easily stripped of its seeds and made ready for use. But it grew sparsely and could not be raised inland. Inland grew the short-fibred cotton, common as a weed, but full of tenacious green seeds that could only be plucked out slowly and with great toil. Big profits could never be made on the scarce sea island cotton. But the green-seed cotton now! If only some swift and easy means could be found to clean it—

Why not, thought Eli. It would only take the proper machine. Catherine was already showing her guests the tambour he had made for her—a kind of frame to hold needlework. If he were skillful enough for this, she was suggesting, why not for some greater task? A few days after he arrived at Mulberry Grove, he wrote later, he "involuntarily happened to be thinking on the subject and struck out a plan for a machine."

Ten days after he turned his attention to the task he had a working model ready, but it was six months before the first gin stood complete, locked in the basement workshop at Mulberry Grove. Catherine, Phineas, and the children watched his progress through the winter and early spring, but none of the neighboring planters was allowed to share the secret until Eli was ready to go north to arrange for a patent.

A previous gin had been in use for cleaning the sea island

cotton, but Eli was only vaguely familiar with it and he had never seen one. It consisted of a pair of wooden rollers grooved lengthwise and rotated by a crank. As the rollers turned in opposite directions the cotton passed between them, and the seeds and impurities caught in the grooves and dropped out.

Eli used the same general idea, but with important differences. His machine had teeth to tear the cotton away from the seeds and an iron guard with slots wide enough to admit the teeth and the cotton fibres caught on them, but too narrow for the green seeds to slip through. Since he could get no sheet iron, he made his guard from iron wire that Catherine's daughter had intended for a bird cage. A set of revolving brushes cleaned the teeth of seeds. As it stood complete it was a simple device, easy to understand and operate, easily made by anyone who knew how to use ordinary blacksmith and carpenter tools. If the crank were turned by one man, it would clean ten times as much cotton as the earlier models and do a better job. But it could also make use of horse and water power, and thus motivated, clean fifty times what it could do if worked by hand.

Only a few of Catherine's friends were allowed to see the gin at first, but they were highly enthusiastic about it and assured Eli that it would make a fortune for him and for the whole South. Green-seed cotton, common and easily grown, would surely become the new staple crop America had been looking for. Clean cotton would flow across the sea to the hungry mills of England. Gold would flow back, helping the new nation to establish its own industries and provide a better life for its people. In May Eli and Phineas drew up an agreement whereby Phineas would supply the money necessary to start manufacturing the gins, Eli would direct the project, and all profits would be mutually shared.

Eli sailed for New York on June first, traveled by stage to Philadelphia, and made his application for a patent to Thomas Jefferson who was then Secretary of State and the official charged with receiving such applications. He paid the fee of thirty dollars and then returned to New York to purchase the materials for setting up a shop in New Haven, keeping careful account of every penny he spent so that he could report it to Phineas. At the Turtle Bay cotton works he had the satisfaction of seeing cotton that he had ginned prove itself clean and of excellent quality. During the summer he worked at New Haven making tools and perfecting a detailed report of his invention to submit to Jefferson. He built a lathe, a drawing block, and other instruments, since he could not purchase them, making himself perhaps the most important pioneer ever to enter the field of machine tool design.

An outbreak of yellow fever slowed the affairs of the capital city that summer and fall, but Jefferson did not leave his post, and corresponded enthusiastically with Eli about the cotton gin. He was interested not only as a government official but as a southern landowner whose estate had a high cotton-growing potential, and he asked many questions. Had the gin been thoroughly tried? How much could it clean on an average of several days if worked by hand? How much would a hand gin cost? Could he purchase one?

Jefferson had gone out of office when Eli finally received his patent from Edward Randolph in March, 1793. By this time Whitney had overcome most of the difficulties that arose when he tried to produce actual working machines from the original model, and now six large gins stood ready for delivery. And none too soon! Phineas Miller had already inserted a notice in the *Gazette of the State of Georgia,* saying that he would "gin any quantity of green-seed cotton on a basis of one pound of cleaned cotton for every five pounds delivered to him in seed." This sounded as if Miller and Whitney were keeping four fifths of the profits, but it would not work out that way because much of the original weight would disappear in cleaning. Their rates were high but not exorbitant. They had devised the machine, put up the capital, and were taking all the risks.

Back at Mulberry Grove, Eli soon found that Phineas had ambitious plans for the business. They would not sell their gins, he had decided. At a cost of four or five hundred dollars, who could afford to purchase one? They would operate them and share the profits with the cotton producers. Already he had 800,000 pounds of cotton on hand, and more planters were clamoring every day to make use of the service. Eli had planned to go to England to get his gin patented there, but instead he hurried back to New Haven to enlarge his workshop and make more gins. Before he left, however, he invented a bagging machine that would enable three slaves to bag six hundred pounds of cotton per day. Meanwhile Phineas sought to locate and buy suitable sites where they could set up ginneries, near the fields of upland cotton, on rivers where water power would be available. By 1796 they had five gins working at Mulberry Grove, ten in Augusta, and nearly a dozen others scattered through Georgia.

It was in May of that year that Catherine finally married the faithful Phineas. And she came loyally to the aid of the partners when they needed her. Eli's workshop burned the year before with a loss of some three thousand pounds. Eli took it grimly, Phineas with enforced good cheer, but they rebuilt in seven months and had twenty-six gins ready to be taken south for installation. This cost money, and other troubles followed. Phineas had speculated in the Yazoo land deal, and when its fraudulence was revealed he had to share the bad reputation that fell to the lot of those who had taken part. Miller and Whitney faced bankruptcy, but Catherine saved them by turning over funds and credit from the Greene estate.

They needed stronger help than Catherine could furnish, however. Three years before it had seemed to Eli Whitney that he faced a future in which he was sure to become not only a rich man and an honored inventive genius, but the benefactor of his country. Now as the century drew to a close he found himself discredited, harassed by debt, his gins standing idle, the cotton they produced unacceptable to the market. His patent had proved no protection from those who wished to steal the design. The Georgia planters resented the high fees charged by Miller and Whitney. But the Whitney gin had changed green-seed cotton into a staple of high value. The farmers had given over thousands of acres to its production, and their widespread need for the gin had become so great that they could no longer respect the rights of the individual. Not only did they manage to construct clumsy gins of their own based on the Whitney design, but they spread the word at home and in England that their "inventions" produced better cotton than the legal machines.

Miller and Whitney had no money to fight this piracy, but Phineas gave stubborn, undaunted attention to it, while Eli, bitter that the laws offered him no protection or redress, shrugged his shoulders and without abandoning his old partner turned to another field of endeavor.

Edward Lyon and Hodgen Holmes were the chief offenders, and Hodgen eventually received a patent for his own gin, though it was later proven to have been based on Whitney's. Some tellers of popular tales liked to recount how Lyon broke into the gin room at Mulberry Grove and carried off the original model, or how he gained access disguised as a woman. As a matter of fact the gin was of such simple construction that anyone who had seen it in operation could make a fair copy if he possessed a little mechanical ability. Even the small boys in the streets of Atlanta knew that it had "teeth which worked through slats and a brush." Miller filed suit after suit against illegal operators but with no success. His enemies went so far as to say that the Whitney gins ruined the cotton and that Eli had not invented them in the first place.

In South Carolina the planters took a different attitude. They believed in the Whitney gin, and eventually made arrangements with Phineas to purchase the right to use it. Wisely now he yielded to good advice and ceased to insist on his firm's sole right to operate the gin. Legal fees absorbed not only his own holdings but much of the Greene property and they lost Mulberry Grove. Moving to another estate of Catherine's called Dungeness, he fought on from there. North Carolina also moved to buy the rights, and eventually Tennessee joined them. The tide had turned and cotton from the patented gins came back into good repute.

Eli made several trips to the south to present helpful testimony in court, proof that he was indeed the gin's inventor, affidavits from the New England mills that they preferred legally ginned cotton. Nevertheless, 1803 proved a bitter year for him. The South Carolina deal held fire and the state threatened to rescind it. Wornout with his struggles, Phineas died of a fever at the age of thirty-nine. Gradually Eli's claims to having invented the gin and being sole owner of it came to be recognized even in Georgia, but by then the patent had run out, and the riches he had dreamed of would have to come from another source if they ever came.

Perhaps he never realized how great an effect he would have on his country. If it was his invention that made cotton king and established the vast economic power of the old South, it was the same simple device of grooved and revolving cylinders that spread and intensified the evil of black slavery and kept it in effect for half a century more. The Yankee handyman can scarcely have thought of that as he toiled in the basement of Mulberry Grove, or when he lay dying in his darkened New Haven bedroom some thirty years later. But he was nowhere near ready for death with the failure of his southern enterprise. He still had fights on his hands, but there would be happiness and successes too, and he surely deserved them.

In the year 1797 Eli Whitney had begun to search for some other venture that would keep him from bankruptcy and make up for his losses on the cotton gin. He could invent and manufacture, but he needed financial support. The rich merchant class had not yet advanced in their economic thinking to the point where they were ready to invest their profits in industry. To the westward land could be had almost for the asking, but Eli did not want land. He wished to engage in some large scale operation, and cast about as he would, he could find nobody with money enough to back him except the federal government in Philadelphia. What did the government need, he asked himself, and by May, 1798, the answer became clear. A war with France threatened in spite of all crusty John Adams could do to avoid it, and the government needed guns. Guns, Eli felt, he could supply.

So he wrote to Oliver Wolcott, a Yale man who had befriended him on other occasions, now Secretary of the Treasury. He asked for a government contract that would enable him to set up a shop and train workers for large scale arms production. He would need $134,000, he said, and in return he would agree to furnish 10,000 muskets within two years and four months, the first delivery to take place in September, 1799. Wolcott received the offer eagerly. Congress had appropriated $800,000 for arms but could find no agency capable of supplying its needs, neither private manufacturers nor the two federal arsenals at Springfield and Harper's Ferry. So Eli got his contract and $5000 advance to put his machines in operation. It was further agreed that his guns should be copies of the Charleville muskets obtained from France during the Revolution, and that United States officials would inspect and approve the finished product, the government also to provide black walnut gunstocks.

It all seemed wonderfully easy, but nothing ever came easy to Eli Whitney except his plentiful ideas and the ability to carry them out in terms of wood and steel. He began at once to seek a good location for his workshop, but troubles plagued him from the start. Loneliness and the need for a wife and family of his own had afflicted him for a long time, but he felt it more keenly now that his two old friends were happily married to each other. Letters hint at marriage plans for him, possibly to one of Catherine's daughters, but nothing came of it.

Homing again to the New Haven area, he finally decided to locate his new workshop in the village of Hamden, near East Rock on the Mill River. High ridges shut off the cold sweep of winds from the north, and the coach road to Hartford ran close by. The river furnished water power and was deep enough below the mill dam so that ships could deliver raw materials there and take the finished guns away. Old farm buildings and a somewhat decayed gristmill could also be utilized. But having chosen this favorable site, his brief good luck ended. First he had trouble in acquiring it and did not actually take possession before mid-September. Then a yellow fever epidemic put Philadelphia under quarantine so that he could not obtain the iron and steel from that market as he had expected to do, nor could the government send the promised gunstocks. A fall drouth lowered the streams, cutting down on the water power he needed for his forges, and then winter struck, early, cold, and cruel, with twelve great storms halting all operations. Furthermore he had trouble raising the added money he would need. By the summer of 1799 he had to apply for more time to complete his first delivery of muskets, and this was finally granted him.

Wolcott and other government officials understood what Whitney was trying to do, but they did not realize the greatness of it, how it would revolutionize every branch of industry. He was trying to produce machine tools that would create standard guns whose parts could be used interchangeably. Before this time there had been no exact standards. Every musket was the work of an individual gunsmith, shaped, constructed and filed to general specifications but with no degree of precision or exactness. Probably no two guns in America were exactly alike, anymore than their owners were exactly alike. Eli Whitney sought to produce guns that were alike—identical in every part. The idea had occurred to others before him, but they had never carried it very far. A Frenchman who died young, various English inventors trying to improve textile machinery, nail-makers in Rhode Island using simple devices on a small scale—but nothing of the magnitude that Whitney had undertaken to achieve. No wonder he needed time.

From the beginning of his task he had proceeded on two established principles. First, he saw the musket he intended to produce, not as one whole, complex machine that must be thrown away if any single part gave out, but as an assembly of small parts, any of which could be replaced if necessary. And secondly, he based his theory of production on machines rather than on men. Handicraft workers could achieve individual excellence, but they could not achieve exact similarity and interchangeableness in their productions. Instead he built machines that would achieve this exactness and taught his men to operate the machines.

His troubles were not over, and he kept having to apply to the government for more time and money. Rivals with interests of their own to serve protested that his guns had flaws and weaknesses, but careful investigation proved that the flaws came from inferior metals and not from slipshod workmanship. Their ramrods might be easily bent, but that fault was common to guns of the time, and Eli's guns were better than any others. When he needed money his friends in New Haven raised ten thousand dollars for his use. Among them was Elizur Goodrich, Jr., and James Hillhouse who planted the famous elms that characterize that city today. Pierpont Edwards also contributed, a wealthy and distinguished man, but free-living to a point that would have shocked his ascetic father, the famous Jonathan.

In 1801 Jefferson's administration was just beginning, and Eli traveled to the new capital, Washington, to demonstrate the various parts of his musket, as well as to discuss his plans for future muskets and their cost. Jefferson gave him his warm friendship and recommended to Virginia that they order arms from the Hamden factory, but Eli did not feel that he could accept further orders until he had completed his original government contract. In the first years of the new century he had to go south again to help close out the business of the cotton gin, but after 1803 he was able to keep up steady deliveries of muskets.

By 1808 he had completed nearly the whole quota and sought to negotiate another government contract. This was necessary in order to keep his workshop running and his men employed. But the federal arsenals were now producing, and Congress had voted to channel armament funds to the individual states. They had no orders to give to Eli Whitney. Nor was he able to retool his shop to turn out any other product. Perhaps he would have to shut down the business altogether. This would not be so serious a matter for him, because he was financially independent now, having made successful investments with Wolcott's brokerage house and the China trade.

But he hated to admit the failure of his enterprise, and he felt a responsibility for his loyal workmen. He had built comfortable stone houses for those with families and provided a boarding house for the bachelors, where a housekeeper and maids served their meals, made their beds, did their washing and mending. Eli himself lived in one of the ancient farm houses with his own servants and a dozen young apprentices, among them the sons of his sister Elizabeth whom he had taken into his care. He did not want to see this little community fall on hard times, and fortunately he did not have to. Arms contracts from New York and Connecticut kept him going until the War of 1812 broke out and the federal government needed his services again.

His health had broken in 1810, and he was to fight painful illness for the rest of his days, but he started eagerly on his second government contract, agreeing to deliver not less than fifteen hundred nor more than three thousand muskets yearly, at the price of thirteen dollars a musket. The British blockade held back some of his supplies, and the War Department set up a shore battery to protect the important Hamden works. But Eli's worst foes did not sail the high seas. They sat behind cluttered desks in Washington.

A shift in authority had placed the Whitney contract under the new Commissary General of Purchases, Captain Callender Irving. Irving and his friend, Marine Wickham, had a musket of their own which they hoped to foist on the United States Army. That it was inferior to Eli's did not deter them. Moreover, Irving hoped to see the national armories increased to the point where they could supply all the arms necessary without employing private contractors. These armories, he thought, should be in charge of one man—and that man, himself. In order to realize his ambitions he began in June, 1813, to attack Whitney.

He withheld funds which should have been paid over according to the contract, and he complained about the muskets already delivered. "The bayonet is two inches too short . . . the butt is too long . . . the barrel is crooked . . . the britch is not water tight." Eli replied patiently that the muskets complied with the model the government had chosen. The feud went on for some time, and Irving did all he could to get the Whitney contract canceled.

He complained that Eli was delivering no guns, and meanwhile the guns piled up at the Hamden works because Irving would send no one to inspect them. Finally he sent Marine Wickham, but Wickham would not reveal to Eli the testing standards that he meant to use. They exchanged angry words and he went away without completing his mission. Eventually the matter went to President Madison who studied the case and saw that Eli received the payments due him. After the peace treaty in 1815, friendly, honest James Carrington became the official inspector for the Hamden establishment. Deliveries after that went according to schedule. Eli improved his machines, especially the triphammer, and built his first milling machine. Other contracts followed, and it was arranged that from January 1, 1824, he would supply the federal government with three thousand muskets every year.

Success, honor, and financial security came to the weary inventor in the last decade of his life, and personal happiness came too. Yale gave him a master's degree, and learned societies welcomed his membership; the state appointed him Justice of the Peace for Hamden. He had talked familiarly with three presidents, Adams, Jefferson, and Madison. And then, on January 6, 1817, his long loneliness came to an end with his marriage to Pierpont Edwards' daughter, Henrietta. The bride was no beautiful young girl, but a thoughtful, intelligent woman of thirty-one, reared in New England's best society. She gave her husband affection, loyalty, three daughters and a son and heir, Eli, Jr.

But by now Eli's health was in serious decline, and his nephew, Eli Whitney Blake, just out of Yale, came to help him, particularly with the final settlement of his interests in the Greene estate, Catherine being now long dead. After 1822, as his bouts of illness and shattering pain became more frequent, scientist to the last, he studied his own medical condition to see if he could find some means of relief.

He and Henrietta had set themselves up in a house on Orange Street in New Haven, while his nephew supervised the works, but Eli never ceased from starting new projects there. He had roads cut and a bridge built, fore runner of the covered bridges that would soon be so popular everywhere. He wrote to his friends about a new process for forging metal and feebly traced the design for a tumbler mill, the last drawing he ever made. To the very day of his death his mind was busy with his work and how to ensure that it would be carried on. When he died in the house on Orange Street, January 8, 1825, he left his family well provided for and his beloved gun works safe in the care of his nephews.

He had been all his days a practical man, not deeply religious, though he attended services at the New Brick Church; not a philosopher, but a genius in the field of applied science and economic operation. He showed no interest in social problems, but our technological society with its companion "Big Business" could not have come into being without the contributions of Eli Whitney.

We can stand by his grave in the quiet Connecticut earth and look back, down the road the builders of New England traveled, in their works if not in the flesh, to be with us today. Slowly in the eye of the mind, New England shrinks from a teeming, industrialized part of a united and powerful nation—back to a tiny fringe of huts on the seacoast of a vast wilderness. When Eli Whitney was born in 1765, Jonathan Edwards had been but a few years dead. Edwards, born in 1703, had listened to the preaching of Cotton Mather. Mather remembered Roger Williams—not favorably—and Williams had shaken hands with Governor Bradford. We are not so many generations off from Elizabethan England after all.

And yet, were William Bradford to walk through Plymouth as we know it, hear the roar of great planes going over in the sky, see the little blue lights of television flickering behind the ancient windows, he would feel less at home than the Connecticut Yankee in Camelot town. He would shake his head, perhaps, and think back to the world he knew and the men who lived with him there. He might say as Elizur Goodrich said in a late letter to Eli Whitney when he spoke of the cotton gin, "These things and these times have passed by, and other folks and other times have succeeded."

And being a devout man, the good Governor might well have added, "And praise the Lord who made it so. Amen."

Index

INDEX